THE COMPLETE
CLAYSHOT

THE COMPLETE CLAYSHOT

Compiled by
Mike Barnes

David & Charles

To Lynne and Tom

A DAVID & CHARLES BOOK

Copyright © Mike Barnes 1993
First published 1993

Mike Barnes has asserted his right to
be identified as author of this work in accordance with
the Copyright, Designs and Patents Act 1988.

A catalogue record for this book is available from the British Library.

ISBN 0 7153 9915 2

Typeset by Angela Kirk, Desk Top Publisher, Exeter
and printed in Great Britain by Redwood Books, Trowbridge
for David & Charles
Brunel House   Newton Abbot   Devon

Contents

Introduction

Trap technology has come a long way – noted
high tower builder and layout designer Ray Wing is
shown here with a LaPorte automatic trap. At the touch of a button
the trap will ride to the top of a 100ft tower and throw clays in the
direction of the operator's choice

For a sport which is now a hundred years old, clay pigeon shooting is some-thing of a new phenomenon. For a very long time it was regarded by many as merely a form of practice for game shooting, and it is only during the last fifteen years that it has developed into a sport in its own right. Now there are something in the region of half a million regular clay shooters; during the last ten years in particular there has been a surge of interest in the sport as people have discovered the joys of shooting clay pigeons. My own involvement came about purely as a result of my work. Initially I joined *Sporting Gun* magazine as a feature writer just after it started—I was a

Opposite:
Clay shooting... a great sport for all ages

trained journalist with no knowledge of clay pigeon shooting. Years earlier, as a teenager, I had shot pigeons but I had never even seen the clay variety.

My first assignment was to visit Fareham Gun Club in Hampshire, armed with the precious little knowledge which I had gleaned during my short time with the magazine. To say that it made a lasting impression is an understatement. Accompanied by photographer and friend Phil Bagnall, we eventually located the place, not quite knowing what to expect. I have since discovered that most clay grounds are never easy to find—you must trust instructions implicitly, or get out of the car and listen, then follow the bangs. What met us was a welcome amidst a hive of activity, everyone bending over backwards to be friendly, a big bustling gathering of people clearly enjoying themselves enormously shooting clay pigeons.

Not only was there clay shooting; to be more precise there was also sporting and trap shooting, and also skeet, it was explained to me. I had my own hands-on initiation of the sport that day: there was a novice stand on which I was given five driven birds and I believe I hit three of them, though it was a bit of a blur at the time (strangely enough just about every other target at some occasion or another has given me problems, but to this date, driven has been a favourite bag-filler). But the lasting impression of the visit, and the main topic of our conversation on the way back to Lincolnshire, was what a great sport this was, and how extraordinary that it was still something of a closed secret. It had been almost like entering another world.

Tackling a pair of crossing targets against a backdrop of rolling countryside

Whether competition or club practice, clay shooting offers so much to participants

That was 1979. Since then clay shooting has lost its 'secret' status; from about 1984 it truly started to gather momentum. There were some major sponsorship promotions in the sport which, while they were criticised for favouring the sport's stars, nevertheless attracted publicity that had previously been absent. They stirred up interest. *Sporting Gun* became involved in a number of big promotions involving both country fairs and clubs, the aim being to stimulate interest and sales. Happily both happened. Jackie Stewart secured coveted television exposure with his celebrity shoots: these featured royalty and stars of stage, screen and sport, people who didn't shoot clay pigeons regularly but nevertheless gave the sport a profile which had previously been absent.

In consequence, clubs mushroomed, memberships soared, and the sport's governing body, the Clay Pigeon Shooting Association, tripled in size. This dramatic growth has not been without its growing pains, however. Some unscrupulous shoot organisers thoughtlessly staged open competitions near urban areas and gave the sport a bad name as a noise nuisance; and there are mercenary individuals who abuse both the CPSA classification system and also local charity shoots in order to win more prizes than their talent deserves. But such as these are the minority, and clay shooting today remains very much as when I experienced that first taste: a world of its own. It is a sport apart, cutting across all social classes, where there is total camaraderie and where most are keen to help others to improve their performance. And in what other sport is it possible for a novice to shoot alongside a British or World Champion? The CPSA runs championships which give every shooter this opportunity.

Rocketing pheasant – and they don't come much higher than this tower at Casa de Campo, in the Dominican Republic, where Michael Rose (ex-West London SG) is the manager

My other regret is that after that first taste at Fareham I became hesitant at shooting in public, and for years was self-conscious about shooting in front of others—as editor of *Sporting Gun* I was concerned about making a fool of myself in front of others! I went to some truly wonderful shoots and never picked up a gun—but when I did, I was given so much conflicting advice that the appearance of every clay pigeon caused any number of crossed wires. I would shoot a pair of targets one way, then do something different for the next; in fact those I did shoot were *despite* my technique rather than as a result of it.

Later, after endless interviews with countless different coaches and top shooters, I was more confused than ever. Nor did it help that I am one of those individuals whose performance in any sport is prone to great variation; football, cricket, tennis are all the same, and snooker highlighted this more than most—I could pot brilliant reds and miss easy blacks. Essentially I now know that in most of my sporting interests I have a decent eye, but not a lot of technique.

Having watched most of our top shots in action over the years I have also come to the conclusion that in shooting, as in any sport, there are always a gifted few—they have an added dimension, certainly most are talented but the winners have a particular will to win, a superior drive and determination. They are also extremely dedicated and their achievements are a fitting

Country fair clayshoots are usually well supported –
and often there is also instruction available

Mike Barnes (centre) with Roger Silcox and Ed Scherer

reward for their effort. Current stars of shooting George Digweed and Stuart Clarke are perfect examples of this; they were both once regular club shooters, but constant application has resulted in their consistently high performances at the top level.

It is a fact of life that most of us do not have that strength of resolve. While we want to excel at our sport and make the most of it with good scores, for various reasons we are unable to give it the necessary commitment. We can, however, learn much from the winners and champions.

I found Robin Scott's contribution to this book very interesting as he has experienced much the same shooting scenario as myself. We have both spoken with a lot of coaches and been given a lot of advice, but unfortunately much of it is conflicting and only serves to confuse because each coach may have his own style. In essence, through the nature of our work, our experience is very much a magnified and compounded version of what happens to anyone who takes up clay pigeon shooting. The beginner will be given a profusion of well intended advice, much of which works beautifully for the provider, but for the recipient it might be at complete odds with other advice given. My own feeling is that individual temperament and responses vary so much that what might be right for one is maybe not so good for another; one person's perception of 'lead' or 'forward allowance' is totally different to another's.

Opposite
**Steve Brightwell shooting a tower bird whilst using the legs
apart stance which has become very popular amongst sporting shooters**

Swing through, tracking, maintained lead—all are different styles and the beginner can be very confused, as indeed I have been over the years. Yet if you take time to observe some of the top sporting shots in action you will see that they tend to borrow a little of each style, depending on the target. In the chapter on general shooting techniques we look at the different styles through the eyes of different contributors; by understanding them it will be possible to go forward. My own feeling is that each shooter will first and foremost grasp the principles of one good, sound, basic technique, then by applying his understanding of other styles and also drawing from the experience of shooting different targets, he will be able to progress.

It is fair to say that every shoot offers the individual something new from which he can learn more about his own shooting. Practice really does make perfect. And if you find yourself slipping into a rut, make a few enquiries to discover the name of a coach who teaches a style which is compatible with your own. Some coaches are very forthright in that *their* way is the *only* way—they will attempt to change you completely. However, although their intentions may be for the good, if you have no international ambitions but merely want to hit more targets on a Sunday morning, they would be better to work on your chosen style to make it more effective. I can speak from experience!

I hope it is not extravagant to claim that this book is quite unlike any others; it is simply that I have sought to present both a picture of the sport as a whole, and by drawing on some of the best known names in it, to give a broad perspective of what clay shooting is all about. And as a final thought, I would also say that some of the nicest people you could ever wish to meet go clay shooting: the contributors to this book most definitely fit into that category, all very respected in their own right, but each ready to share their thoughts and experiences with anyone who cares to listen. I am obviously grateful for their contributions, and hope that readers enjoy the book as much as I did when putting it together.

Mike Barnes
Morton, Lincolnshire, 1993

PART 1
A LOOK BEHIND
THE SPORT

1
Guns: Making the Right Choice

Mike Barnes

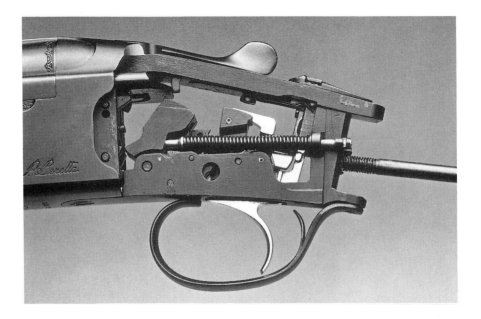

The internal workings of an over-under

By the very nature of the sport, all of the contributors to this book discuss guns—the gun, after all, is an important variable upon which your performance depends. Most of the other variables are human fallibilities, so it is important that your choice of gun is correct: this is perhaps an appropriate point at which to consider some of the basic requirements to look for when buying a gun. And I am not referring to either condition or internal mechanics—Desmond Mills discusses these very ably elsewhere (see p. 153). I am referring to understanding the basics of gun design, and what type of gun you will be looking for.

As all coaches will point out, only by understanding what you do will any real progress start to take place; and the same applies to that all-important investment, the gun. It is fair to say that while in general terms the design of the over-under shotgun has changed precious little in eighty years, the quality and choice of models now available is unparalleled in the history of the sport. I say the over-under shotgun, as this is by far the most popular barrel configuration used for clay pigeon shooting. Second is the semi-automatic, and third the side-by-side shotgun.

Top competitors use guns which are readily available to all of us. They never, ever use side-by-sides for clay pigeon shooting, for no other reason than that they find them more difficult to shoot with. There is no prejudice involved, indeed I am sure that many would like to shoot with a pretty English gun; but the simple fact is that they could never produce winning scores with them.

The principal reason for this is that the side-by-side was evolved for game shooting; it is light, quick and responsive, and ideal for driven game shooting. But the clay shooter will need all of these qualities from a gun, and more—shooting a pair of going-away targets with a side-by-side would be difficult. Because these guns are light, their barrels tend to jump in the air on firing the first shot. On the swing-through of a driven game bird this doesn't matter, but on a precision going-away or quartering shot, such a gun is virtually uncontrollable. The light gun is also much more punishing in terms of recoil, which in turn leads to flinching and fatigue.

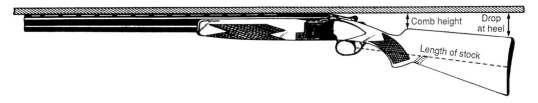

An over-under, showing the areas crucial to gun fit

The single sighting plane of the over-under gives it a further advantage over the side-by-side. Interestingly, while semi-automatics are very popular in the USA they are much less so in this country; I am not sure of the reason why. The only top shooter of note who uses one is the twice World Champion, Duncan Lawton; others cite reasons of reliability, but I suspect it is more because the look of a gun is more important to British shooters than their counterparts in probably any other country in the world.

A lot of overseas clay target shooters look simply to how a gun performs. This is obviously important in Britain too, but most of us also like to see a nice piece of walnut on a gun and perhaps some engraving. Pump guns can be used, but my feeling is that there is enough to think about when shooting without having to 'pump' a gun between shots!

So, which make do you choose, and what type of gun? Firstly, the make of gun is down to personal preference. The most important part of the equation is to buy the best you can afford—and if you can't afford a new gun, then think in terms of secondhand. Guns are durable items, particularly if well looked after, and most gun shops will have a good selection of used models by the better manufacturers.

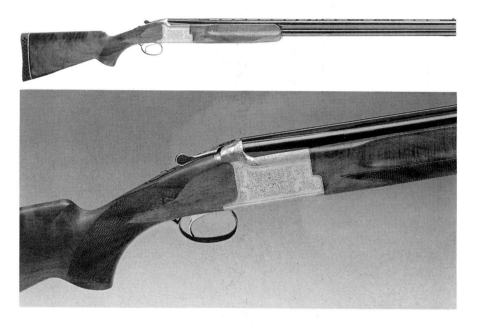

The Miroku 3800, the most popular gun for DTL

Browning, Beretta, Miroku, Perazzi—all of these are top-line makes. On the secondhand shelf you will see names no longer in production such as Winchester and Nikko, which again are very good guns. There are also some decent mid-price models such as Lanber, Lincoln and Fabarm; but beware of the real cheapies. Buy a well known make and you will have a gun that is less likely to let you down, is much easier to handle, and has less recoil; in the longer term it will represent a sound financial investment. It is a fact that models made by most of the well known names appreciate in value over a period of time; you only have to look at the pages of a shooting magazine which is six or seven years old to see how the prices have risen. And my feeling is that this will continue to happen. Moreover Beretta has led the way in the investment of hi-tech machinery to produce guns of very high quality at affordable prices, and other companies have followed suit. Added to which, during the boom in clay shooting a lot of discount mail order shops sold guns at very cheap prices in order to retain their volume of sales. Now the volume has dropped off, the manufacturers, importers and retailers will all be looking for better margins. Note the word 'importers'— sadly no over-unders are made in this country, other than very expensive (£30,000–£60,000) London guns by the likes of Purdey and Holland & Holland.

So basically, investing in a gun mostly represents a good long-term investment.

As for choosing, this will be down to the individual. The 1992 European FITASC Sporting Championship showed a cross-section of guns used: winner George Digweed shoots a Beretta, Silver medallist A.J. Smith a Classic Doubles, and bronze medallist Stuart Clarke a Miroku. George

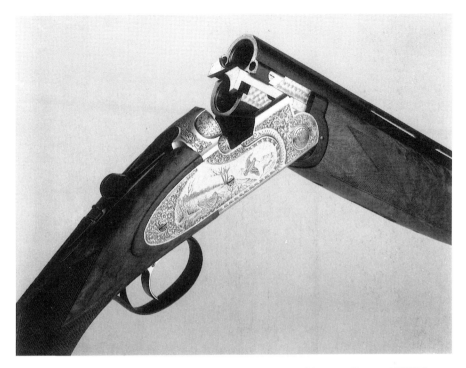

Some shooters enjoy owning a nicely engraved gun, in this case a Beretta 687EELL

Digweed started his career with a Miroku, A.J. Smith has previously been successful with both Browning and Winchester, and Stuart Clarke previously shot a Beretta! In other words, it's safe to settle on any of these makes. Speak with a few regular shooters; they will either swear by one particular make, or will admit to changing brands in search of improved performance.

What type of gun? Sporting, skeet or trap gun? And what are the differences? For all-round shooting, the sporting multi-choke is the perfect answer, including skeet shooting. Before the advent of screw-in chokes, the skeet gun was very popular—shortish (26/27in) barrels, open chokes and quick handling for close-range skeet targets. But now with a multi-choke, unless you happen to be a specialist skeet shooter, it is quite possible to use one gun for both disciplines.

For trap shooting, however, you will need a trap gun. This will differ from the sporting model by virtue of its being heavier, with slightly longer stock with smaller comb height, a stock heel pad, and barrels of minimum 30in length. Some trap guns have screw-in chokes, but these are a small minority; most will have fixed choking of 3/4 and full.

So, what is choke and comb? Choke and its effects are dealt with in more detail in David Garrard's chapter (see p. 25). But essentially, choke is the amount of constriction in the end of a shotgun barrel which dictates the spread of the shot, ranging from improved cylinder and skeet for close targets (a wide pattern of shot is established at close range) to full choke for long-range targets (a tight pattern which is slow to spread and is still dense

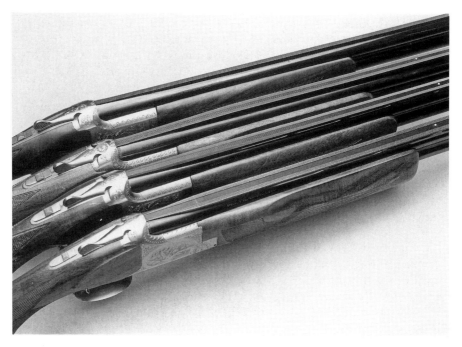

**Four Browning guns with different ribs: (from the top) narrow game rib;
standard competition rib; raised ventilated rib; Broadway rib**

with no gaps at a range of 40 yards. The consistently effective clay-breaking range of a shotgun does not go much beyond 50–60 yards (and for most of us it is much less!).

On a round of sporting clays, which can vary from close-driven to long-range quartering targets, the option of changing chokes, as with a screw-in multi-choke gun, is attractive. Some prefer to stick with one combination for the whole round, 1/4 and 1/2 for instance. But with a multi-choke the decision lies with the shooter. A normal selection of five chokes is improved cylinder, 1/4, 1/2, 3/4 and full. Improved and 1/4 will be a pretty versatile pairing for average club sporting targets, and also fine for the skeet range.

Comb height is one of the terms used in relation to the configuration of a gun stock. While it doesn't pay for the novice to get too wrapped up in detail, it is crucial that he understands the basics of guns and fit. Comb height is in fact very important because it dictates the level of your eye in relation to the barrel. When the gun is properly mounted, your eye should be looking straight down the barrel rib and seeing just a little of it. Comb height is the distance between an imaginary line drawn parallel with the rib, and the top of the stock immediately beneath your eye. This point on the stock is known as the 'comb'.

Trap guns have a smaller degree of comb height, because all trap targets are retreating from the gun and rising slightly; with increased comb height, the shooter can keep the target in view knowing that his gun will shoot slightly higher than a conventional sporting multi-choke (which will normally throw 1/3 of the pattern on or below the target, and the remainder above). Sadly, there are 'shops' or dealers who have been known to sell trap guns to novices seeking their first gun for general sporting shooting; the object of this exercise is purely to fill their coffers by moving a gun that has been gathering dust on the shelf. The other gun to avoid when in such a situation is the multi-choke game (or field) model. These guns are fine for pigeon shooting, but not clay pigeons—they are too light, have less capacity for recoil, and are more difficult to control on a demanding clay layout.

Such individuals who offload their game and trap models on unsuspecting customers are happily not the norm; make sure you visit a good, reputable gun shop when making your purchase. They will be happy to give good advice, as obviously there is nothing better for trade than satisfied customers.

The other phrase you may hear is 'drop at heel': the distance between the imaginary line and the heel of the stock.

Further important factors to consider are length of stock and cast. If a stock is too long it will be difficult to mount; if it is too short it will cause bruising, and this makes it difficult to control the gun properly.

Cast is the degree to which the stock needs to be 'bent out' from the line of the barrels in order to allow the eye to fall into the correct position immediately behind the barrels. Normally only a slight amount of cast is

Most sporting over-unders nowadays are fitted with multi-chokes which simply screw into the end of the barrel and give the shooter a number of options

necessary and an off-the-shelf gun should meet most requirements, although certain refinements may be necessary as your level of performance and expectations rise. A gun must fit reasonably at the outset—as your standards improve, the precision of fit will become increasingly important.

Beware of having a sharp point at the heel of the stock—this is particularly uncomfortable for ladies, and digs sharply into the body. In all aspects the gun must fit easily into the face and shoulder on mounting; when practising mounting it should be possible to close your eyes, then open them to discover that the barrels are exactly where you want them to be. This barrel/eye relationship is absolutely vital—in effect, your eye is the back sight. If the relationship is less than perfect, then it will be impossible to shoot well and you will probably develop head-lifting problems—that is, you lift your head to check the target as you are about to shoot, which results in unaccountable misses. The problem is that few head-lifters ever realise they are doing it—though capture the offenders on video film and then show them the evidence, and this will bring them back to reality with a sharp jolt.

Furthermore, if the gun isn't mounted in the correct position, then bruising of the cheek and/or shoulder can easily result. If the fit and mount are correct, then recoil is not generally a worry.

Triggers are very important, but will not normally be a consideration when buying any of the top makes; these all have good trigger pulls. However, if you look at a cheaper make, you will find that the extent of the trigger pull can vary enormously, and most are too heavy. I have tried guns where it is almost impossible to pull the trigger, and guns that have been brand-new out of the box, no question of having seized, just simply evidence of bad manufacture and a total lack of quality control.

Ported barrels reduce both muzzle flip and recoil

A trigger pull is the amount of resistance or force necessary in order to fire the gun. There needs to be sufficient resistance to prevent the gun being fired accidently, but not so much as to prevent the taking of the shot when the brain sends the appropriate impulse through the body. Normal trigger pulls are around 4lb, although a cheap gun may be double that; the consequence of a heavy pull is that you lose timing completely. In the taking of the shot the pulling of the trigger is done almost subconsciously—if there is resistance on the trigger then the sequence is broken.

It goes without saying that a well-looked-after gun is less likely to let you down, will give more pleasure to the user, and in the longer term will protect your investment. It is easy enough to keep a gun clean and lightly oiled; properly looked after, it will last a lifetime.

Other Important Essentials

While the gun is the most important and by far the most expensive piece of any shooter's equipment, it represents, as we have said, an investment which will hold its price and appreciate. Therefore having spent your money wisely, you can indulge yourself in one or two extras which form part of the essential kit for the complete clay pigeon shooter. The four most important items are shooting vest, ear defenders, shooting glasses and hat.

The first two of these are absolutely essential. Only in a sleeveless shooting vest will those all-important factors of gun-fit be allowed free rein. The two vital aspects of a shooting vest are that it allows unrestricted movement around the shoulder area, and the leather shoulder patch means that the gun can be mounted consistently without fear of catching on either cloth material, pocket, button or other obstruction. It's a fact that your gun only has to catch once on mounting, and the seeds of doubt are immediately sown. After this has happened it is virtually impossible to shoot freely and naturally as your mind will always be subconsciously concerning itself with the possibility of a mismount and you will be distracted from the job in hand.

Ear defenders are today accepted as part and parcel of clay shooting. Where only five or six years ago relatively few shooters wore ear muffs, today most are aware of the dangers of damaged hearing—you only have to observe two longstanding shots engaged in conversation, turning their heads sideways to one another in order to hear. Don't let it happen to you. Again, there is an excellent selection on the market, of either plugs or muffs. I confess to being a slow learner in this respect, and for years I shot without any protection. I found the buzzing unpleasant with plugs in situ, and when I wore muffs I found them distracting as the stock tended to catch them on mounting. This more than anything highlighted the inadequacies of my gun-mount! I have now, as a direct result of wearing earmuffs, corrected my gun-mount.

Shooting glasses are a more important piece of shooting kit than many realise. Their usefulness when shooting targets into bright sunlight is obvious, and increasingly people are aware of the advantages of a coloured lens which helps to improve visibility in poor conditions, or to pick out fluorescent targets for those of us who find it difficult to come to terms with luminous orange (me included). But the key factor offered by glasses is that of eye protection. Eyes are precious, and they don't repair easily—it would take only a tiny piece of broken clay to do untold damage, and this could come from a low-driven target, or station one low house on skeet, or a bit which has blown in the wind. Broken clays have sharp, jagged edges. You may go through your whole shooting career without being hit by a piece—or it could happen next week.

For the very same reason it is advisable to wear a shooting cap. The cap itself protects the head, the peak cuts out fierce light and also protects the eyes and forehead.

The other piece of equipment necessary is a set of waterproofs. You can buy these to match your chosen brand of gun—Browning or Beretta—or you can get a pair from the local gunshop or sports shop. The thin water-proof material will enable you to carry on shooting in your skeet vest, whereas a waxproof will jeopardise your gun-mount. This is not being unnecessarily fussy. You may conjure images of pheasant shooters who always wear heavy clothing, but again, the difference is that most of their shots are similar, *ie* driven. An adjustment can be made to accommodate all of their shooting during a cold and wet day. But when clay shooting, taking a difficult on-report pair of quartering targets is totally dependent on the kind of precise gun-mounting that it is impossible to guarantee when wearing a waxproof jacket.

A gun safe is a one-off purchase which I feel is a must. You will also have bought a cleaning kit for your gun, and the only other item of expenditure which I feel is necessary is that of joining the Clay Pigeon Shooting Association. You may or may not wish to compete in the big champi-onships—though I feel that this is a pleasure worth savouring by every shooter, if only once a year—but the package of £2 million insurance, the bi-monthly *Pull!* magazine, and the opportunity of taking part in registered shoots, are all very attractive. There are also a number of courses of various kinds available to members. And as time goes by, membership of the sport's parent body is going to become increasingly important.

There used to be a pre-conception among many shooters that the CPSA was exclusively for the top shots, and had nothing to offer the club shooter. But this is no longer the case—it is the club shooter who matters most to the future of the sport. For details write to: The CPSA, 107 Epping New Road, Buckhurst Hill, Essex IG9 5TQ; tel 081 505 6221.

2
Cartridges

David Garrard

As a result of years of competitive research and development the modern shotgun cartridge has reached such a high level of reliability and consistency that a first-class performance can be assumed as a matter of course. Although it is most unlikely that a faulty cartridge lies behind a 'miss' recorded on the score-card, a close look at its construction is a helpful background to successful shooting and an understanding of ballistics.

The diagrams show the longitudinal cross-section of two modern cartridges. Diagram (a) shows the most frequently found form, in which the contents are enclosed in a plastic tube with parallel walls of constant thickness (.22–.23in). This tube is manufactured by the Reifenhauser process which confers the necessary elasticity and flexibility to the material. The tube is set in a metal head, normally of rust-proofed mild steel but occasionally of the more expensive but totally rust-resistant brass. In the centre of this head is set the battery-cup primer (as shown in the separate diagram c). At the bottom of the tube, where it is set into the head, is a plastic base-wad which locks the tube into the head and provides a seal to prevent the escape of the high pressure powder gases when the cartridge is fired. Immediately above the base-wad lies the charge of gunpowder, normally running 20–25 grains in weight. This is the power-house of the cartridge, and when ignited provides the energy to propel the shot charge up the barrel at such velocity that it will eventually fall to the ground at least 200 yards away—all from a level teaspoon of harmless-looking little grains.

Seated on the powder is the wad, which in modern ammunition is a

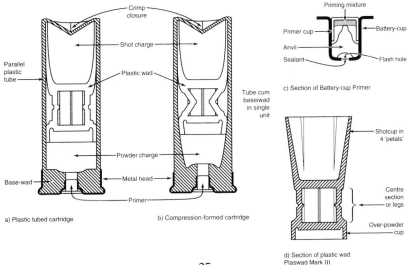

a) Plastic tubed cartridge

b) Compression-formed cartridge

c) Section of Battery-cup Primer

d) Section of plastic wad Plaswad Mark III

plastic unit comprising three parts (see d). The over-powder cup seals off the high-pressure powder gases and thus maximises their propulsive energy. The centre section collapses progressively under the thrust of the powder gases, and in this way cushions the shot charge and the shooter's shoulder from the recoil effects of the accelerating shot charge. The extent and rate at which this collapse occurs has a very significant effect on the pressure developed in the cartridge. The upper portion of the plastic wad comprises a 'cup', usually of four separate 'petals' which enclose the shot charge. Its function is to protect the shot pellets during their passage up the barrel, from abrasion on the barrel walls. Full weight, unworn and undistorted pellets such as these retain maximum energy and, pursuing a direct flight, contribute to dense, uniform patterns.

The litter problem presented by the accumulation of plastic wads is of no account on full-time shooting grounds, but can be a serious objection to shooting at informal venues such as country fairs. At such sites the use of fibre wadding is usually made compulsory since these vegetable fibre components soon disintegrate and rot down, leaving the field clear of plastic. Such fibre wadding was in universal use prior to the introduction of plastic wadding thirty years ago. It normally results in rather more open patterns than the plastic equivalent, but that is a handicap shared by all competitors.

The shot charge contained within the plastic cup is arguably the most important constituent of the cartridge, as it alone is responsible for actually breaking the target. In modern clay cartridges the weight of the charge is restricted by regulation to 1oz (28g). Trap loads are composed of 340 pellets (No 7/2.4mm) or 400 pellets (No 7$\frac{1}{2}$/2.3mm). Sporting shooters often depend on slightly smaller-sized shot such as No 8 (2.2mm), while skeet competitors shooting at around 20 yards range with open-bored barrels depend almost exclusively on No 9 shot (2.0mm). In fact competitive skeet rules do not permit shot any larger than 9.

If good quality, consistent patterns are to be recorded, the individual shot pellets should be, as near as possible, of identical spherical shape and size, although absolute uniformity cannot be attained by the drop process of manufacture. Pellet hardness is another important quality, as really hard shot resists deformation in the breech and hence prints the close patterns essential for success in all the clay disciplines. Hardness is measured by dropping a weight on individual shot pellets from a known height; the resultant reduction in diameter is expressed as a percentage of the original diameter and known as 'crush value'. The popular No 7 shot should, for instance, exhibit a crush value of 32–28 per cent which can be attained if the lead is alloyed with 2–3 per cent antimony. Anything less is unsatisfactory for consistent, successful clay-busting. Cartridge loaders are generally well aware of the necessity of loading good quality, hard shot, and really first-class stuff is now the norm.

The mouth of the cartridge, immediately above the shot, is closed with a crimp closure, normally with six but occasionally with eight sections. A tightly formed crimp is essential if it is to offer sufficient resistance to the expanding powder gases to ensure a clean powder burn, and hence the development of optimum velocity of the shot charge. Modern cartridges are rarely wanting in this respect.

The other cartridge shown at diagram B is based on a compression-formed case; such a case is formed from a single plastic slug by a high compression process in a steel die. The result is a one-piece case in which the tube is combined with the plastic base; it has a fairly marked internal taper. This system of manufacture produces strong, durable cases, ideal for reloading. Compression-formed cases are all of American origin, produced under patents held by the Winchester and Remington companies. The contents of the compression-formed case are identical with those of the plastic-tubed case, apart from slight modifications of the powder charge and possibly of wad design.

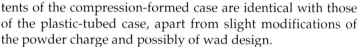

A third, relative newcomer to the cartridge scene is the Activ cartridge. This is essentially similar to the plastic-tubed case but is manufactured in two parts, a Reifenhauser tube being heat-welded to an injection-moulded base. There is no metal head, the rim of the case being reinforced with a circular steel insert. Again a very durable case, ideally suited to re-loading.

The Activ case: note the absence of a metal head

Working function of the cartridge

A brief account of just how the cartridge works is appropriate before considering ballistics and patterns and so on. Action starts when the firing pin strikes the central cap of the primer, thus compressing the priming compound sharply against the anvil. The compound detonates, producing a white-hot high-pressure flame which permeates and ignites the powder charge. The size of this igniting flame is matched to the powder in use, large enough to give efficient ignition of the powder and to avoid poor, erratic ballistics, yet not so large as to give rise to excessive pressures with consequent open patterns.

The gases from the burning powder expand very rapidly, exerting pressure on the base of the wad which, as it collapses, transfers the thrust to the shot charge; once the inertia of this is overcome, it bursts through the crimp closure and is accelerated up the barrel. Within 8 inches or so the shot is travelling at around 1,000ft/sec and clears the muzzle at 1,400–1,500ft/sec in modern clay cartridges.

It is important to note that the expanding powder gases will drive the gun backwards with the same momentum as they drive the shot/wad charge forwards. This is responsible for recoil, which is a product of the weight of the shot/wad charge x the maximum velocity that it reaches. A simple little formula expresses this relationship:

X=weight of charge x max velocity of charge=weight of gun x velocity of recoil of gun. X produces 100–110 units of momentum from a 1oz charge, exiting the muzzle at 1,500ft/sec. If the recoil velocity of the gun is to be kept within 16ft/sec, the maximum for comfortable shooting, then the weight of the gun must lie within 100/16–110/16lb=6¼–7lb. As most clay-shooting guns weigh around 7½–8½lb recoil is not normally a problem—unlike game shooting where the use of lightweight guns can cause difficulties. Those allergic to arithmetic can be safely guided by the old rule of 6lb of gun (at least) to each 1oz of shot.

Ballistics

There are two main features of cartridge performance that are of essential interest to the shooter. Firstly is the *pressure* developed within the gun which, acting on the base of the wad, propels the charge up the barrel and into flight towards the target. The *velocity* so attained is the second essential and is of the greatest practical interest.

Pressure

The pressure developed within the breech must be high enough to propel the charge at an effective velocity, yet not so high as to damage or even burst the gun. Any chance of this happening is virtually eliminated by the compulsory proof-testing of all guns sold in Great Britain, since all 12-bore, 2¾in chambered guns so proved are marked with either the *maximum service charge*—1¼oz if made prior to 1955—or the *maximum service pressure*, 3¼tons/sq in, if made from 1955 onwards. Imported guns are marked with the *actual proof pressure*, which for 2¾in (70mm) guns is 900kg/sq cm which is equivalent to the max service load/pressure given above. A very recent development concerns the implementation of the CIP proof regulations which now apply in Great Britain and throughout Europe. These require that all 12-bore guns other than magnums be proved at 850 bars; they are then suitable for use with cartridges that develop an average 1in pressure not in excess of 650 bars.

All this may appear to be rather complex and worrying to the novice to the sport. However, he should take heart. All he has to do to play safe is to ensure that his cartridges are labelled as being in 2¾in (67½mm) cases—*no longer*—and that they either bear the CIP logo or are stated to be suitable in guns with a max service charge of 1¼oz or a max service pressure of 3¼ tons/sq in; alternatively that they have been proved at 900kg/sq cm. No real problem here, as very effective clay cartridges can be loaded within these limits, a majority not exceeding 500–600 bars.

Velocity

There are two quite different methods of defining the velocity of the shot charge from a shotgun. In Great Britain the traditional description, still adhered to by a majority of loaders, is the observed velocity. This is the average velocity over the first 20 yards (or metres) of flight. It has the advantage in that it at least refers to the velocity of the pellets when they are travelling as individual pellets, whereas the muzzle velocity (favoured in the USA) refers to the velocity of the shot charge as it emerges from the muzzle as a solid slug.

There is scope for confusion here. Some loaders, hoping no doubt to impress potential customers, quote the muzzle velocity—1,500ft/sec, for example; it reads so much better than, 1,150ft/sec, although both refer to an identical pellet velocity! As a rough rule, if the quoted velocity exceeds 1,200ft/sec it is almost certainly the muzzle velocity, and not the observed figure. In fact loaders only rarely indicate the velocity developed by their ammunition, and shooters have either to rely on their judgement or on reviews in the sporting press.

Originally all shotgun ammunition was loaded to an observed velocity of approx 1,050ft/sec=1,300ft/sec at the muzzle, with trap loads often loaded to a lower level in the interests of pattern quality. All this is now altered. The introduction of modern progressive powders, plastic wadding and so on, means that cartridges can be loaded to much higher velocities, yet at well within max service pressure limits. Clay shooters appear to have an insatiable appetite for fast cartridges, fed by suppliers who often imply that 'faster is better'. A personal view is that an observed velocity of 1,100–1,150ft/sec is ample for all purposes. Above this level the increase in pellet striking energy and the reduction in time of flight are really so insignificant as hardly to justify the inevitable increase in recoil and noise which all add up towards the end of a big day.

Patterns

Shooters are aware that after exiting the muzzle as a solid slug, the shot charge is soon dispersed by air pressure and thereafter travels forward as a cloud or column of individual pellets. This cloud lengthens and expands as it travels down-range, and for instance could be around 4 feet in length at 30 yards from the muzzle, running 27–45 inches in diameter according to the degree by which the barrel is choked. A cross-sectional picture of this shot column can be obtained by firing at a vertical painted plate or sheet of paper on which the pellets will make their mark. This agglomeration of pellet marks is known as the pattern, made by that particular charge from the barrel in use. An analysis of this pattern will give a very accurate picture of its potential for breaking the target. The first step in arriving at this analysis is to describe a circle 30 inches in diameter, centred on the densest part of the pattern which can normally be identified quite easily. The pellets contained within this circle are then counted and expressed as a percentage of the total pellets in the charge. This figure is termed the *percentage density*.

If, for instance, the charge comprised 1oz of No 7 shot (340 pellets), a count of 204 pellets in the 30in circle would represent a pattern of:

$$\frac{204 \times 100}{340} = 60 \text{ per cent density}$$

Similarly a count of 238 pellets = 70 per cent density, and a count of 170 pellets = 50 per cent. Individual patterns vary by up to 10 per cent each side of average, and for this reason it is essential to record at least five patterns of any gun/cartridge combination—ten patterns is better. A total variation of less than 10 per cent is not uncommon, with 20 per cent as the maximum acceptable limit. These variations apply to the average of all the patterns recorded. The part that choke plays in determining pattern percentage has already been touched on, and must be considered in greater detail before considering patterns and their assessment in depth.

Choke consists of a narrowing of the bore of the barrel immediately behind the muzzle with the intention of concentrating the shot pellets as they leave the barrel and thus causing them to print a pattern which is more dense or concentrated than that from an unchoked or true cylinder barrel. Very occasionally barrels are trumpet or recessed choked with the object of opening up the patterns; normally, however, the greater the degree of choke the denser the resultant patterns, as the following table shows:

TABLE 1

Pattern percentage in 30in circle							
	inches				*Range in yards*		
Choke	Normal constriction	20	25	30	35	40	45
Full	.040	100	100	100	84	70	59
¾ choke	.030	100	100	91	77	65	55
½ choke	.020	100	94	83	71	60	50
¼ choke	.010	100	87	77	65	55	46
Imp cyl	.005	92	82	72	60	50	41
True cyl	Nil*	80	69	60	49	40	33

*Note that to achieve the percentages shown, a very slight degree of choke is often called for, say .002–.003in.

These are nominal patterns, from which individual combinations of gun and cartridge may well vary quite widely when put to the test on the pattern plate—the only satisfactory method of making this important determination.

Originally barrels carried a fixed choke that was (and is) fine for game shooting but lacks the flexibility that the all-round clay shooter requires. This need has been met by the introduction of variable choke tubes that screw into or onto the gun muzzles; a very useful facility that is strongly recommended to all competitors.

Shot sizes As Table 1 shows, pattern density varies directly with the degree of choke and the distance at which the shot is taken. As the latter is usually known within close limits, the choice of choke is facilitated. The other factors which fix the degree of choke are the size of the target and the number of pellets in the charge, and this in turn is determined by the size of the shot pellets in use.

A standard clay target 'edge on' to the shooter presents a very small

The shooter should remember that there is a shot string; coaches advise beginners to 'miss in front', knowing that there is a shot string to compensate inaccuracies

mark, requiring the use of small shot combined with a marked degree of choke to produce the dense patterns necessary for consistent kills. Years of experience have demonstrated that the following shot sizes are best suited to the disciplines shown, and there is nothing to be gained by departing from them.

Discipline	Shot size
Trap, all forms	No 7 (2.4mm) = No 7½ (Italian and USA)
	No 7½ (2.3mm) = No 8 (Italian and USA)
Sporting clays	Nos 7 and 7½ can be combined with No 9, the latter for the smaller targets such as minis and targets off the tower. A widely used, all-round size is No 8 (2.2mm)
Skeet	No 9 (2.0mm) is used universally = No 9½ by some Italian loaders

Note the scope for confusion caused by the existence of differing scales of shot sizes. Fortunately most loaders quote the pellet diameter in millimetres, which is the best guide to shot size.

Pattern Assessment   A detailed study of the arrangement of pellets within patterns shows that their apparent random distribution in fact follows a recognisable mode; all patterns thus show a concentration of pellets towards the centre which increases in degree with the increase in percentage density. This results in an overall pattern of pellet distribution which is known as Gaussian and is subject to mathematical analysis which can determine within close limits the likely performance of the pattern on a defined target. The latest and most up-to-date work on this subject has been done by Dr Roger Giblin at University College, London, and it is on rules formulated and kindly supplied by him that the assessments of the patterns that follow are made. It is assumed here that:

1 The pellet intercepting area of an edge-on standard clay target as presented at virtually all clay disciplines other than overhead 'birds' is 6sq in. The minimum area is just under 4sq in but an element of tilt normally increases this to the assumed value.
2 An average strike of three pellets is required to register a kill on a standard clay target. This should ensure an 80 per cent chance of a two-pellet strike. This is a difficult matter to decide, but the figure suggested fits in with experience in competition.

Trap Shooting

This discipline involves shooting at a rapidly retreating target thrown at defined angles. Very high scores are the norm, requiring an extremely consistent performance from the shooter. The tiny target at longish range demands very close patterns with correspondingly heavy choke if the necessary level of performance is to be attained.

TABLE 2

Typical Patterns for Trap Shooting					
	40yd 70%		35yd 80%		30yd 90%
	no 7	no 7½	no 7	no 7½	
Hits at pattern centre	3/4	4	4/5	5/6	6/7	7/8
Max diam pattern (in inches) for 3 pellet average strike	10/11	14	15	18	17	19

*Note All recorded with a full choke barrel, 1oz charges of No 7 (2.4mm 340 pellets) and No 7½ (2.3mm 400 pellets). (The target is assumed to present a pellet intercepting area of 6sqin with a 3-pellet average 'strike' as the minimum for a recorded 'kill'.)

An inspection of the bottom line of Table 2 confirms that really straight shooting is called for, the effective 'killing' circle being some 17–19in at 30 yards and only 10in at 40 yards. It is clearly an advantage to take the targets as early as possible, say within 30–35 yards, full choke always being essential. Some trap ammunition will print denser patterns than those suggested and a properly conducted patterning session to identify such cartridges could be a worthwhile exercise, since every pellet counts in this discipline. Note that no 7½ shot confers a slight advantage in terms of hits on the target and on permissible aiming error, but it lacks the striking energy of no 7 which could be decisive at the longer ranges. Personal choice based on experience in the field will be the best guide to shot size for trap shooting, where faith could well be the deciding factor!

Sporting Shooting

Targets at extreme range should not be a problem here as most shooting consists of pairs with the second target on report. Crossers, quartering targets, oncomers, retreating and overhead 'birds' as well as 'rabbits' all feature in this discipline using standard, midi, mini and battue targets. A versatile performance is therefore required, and this is favoured by choking that confers reasonable scope for errors of pointing at the ranges and targets concerned. The choice lies between 1/4 and 1/2 choke, both of which feature in Table 3 in conjunction with No 8 shot. This is a useful all-round size, but No 9 has a part to play at the shorter ranges, especially where the tiny mini targets are concerned.

TABLE 3

Typical Sporting Patterns						
	35yd		30yd		25yd	
	1/2c (70%)	1/4c (65%)	1/2c (80%)	1/4c (75%)	1/2c (90%)	1/4c (85%)
Hits at pattern centre	4/5	4	6	5	9	7
Max diam pattern (in inches) for 3-pellet average strike	17	14	21	18	20	22

*Note Recorded with 1/2 and 1/4 choke barrels at three ranges. A 1oz charge of No 8 (2.2mm 450 pellets/oz). (The target is assumed to present a pellet intercepting area of 6sq in with a 3-pellet average strike as the minimum for a recorded 'kill'.)

At the longest range, 35 yards, 1/2 choke clearly has the edge in terms of pellet strikes and diameter of effective pattern. These advantages lessen as range diminishes, with 1/4 choke showing up very well at 25 yards and below. For all-round sporting shooting there is obviously much to be said for employing both borings, with the 1/2-choke barrel reserved for the longest of the usual pairs. Shot size has already been touched upon.

Skeet Shooting

Here, range is virtually fixed at 20-odd yards or below for on comers. No 9 shot delivers ample pellet-striking energy at these short ranges, and gives plenty of pattern (pellet counts) from really lightly choked barrels. In Table 4, 1/4-choke and true cylinder barrels are compared.

TABLE 4

Typical Skeet patterns		
	1/4 choke	True Cyl
Hits at pattern centre	15	8
Max pattern diam (in inches) for 3-pellet average strike	21	23.5

*Note Recorded at 21 yards with true cylinder and 1/4 choke barrels. 1oz No 9 shot (2.0mm 580 pellets/oz). (The target is assumed to present a pellet intercepting area of 6sq in with a 3-pellet average strike as the minimum for a recorded 'kill'.)

At the stipulated range, the 1/4-choke barrel give a real smoking performance over a slightly smaller optimum diameter pattern than the true cylinder boring. At the shorter distances the true cylinder barrel could provide more scope for pointing errors with plenty of striking power, and could be the best all-round choice for novice skeeters.

Experienced Class A competitors could prefer the decisive kills consequent on using the tighter 1/4-choke barrel. There are occasional conditions when even more choke could be required, for example when a stiff crosswind pushes the targets (especially from the high house) out to approaching the 30-yard mark. The extra pattern (pellet strikes) provided by a 1/2-choke barrel should be the answer here—a good example of the flexibility offered by variable choke tubes. Individual preference and performance will determine the best choice of choke for skeet shooting, bearing the above evidence in mind.

No mention has been made of patterns for clay targets 'off the tower'. Such standard targets present a pellet intercepting area of 14sq in and are not a difficult ballistic proposition compared with the more usual trap/sporting kind. Many of the most experienced shots use nothing but No 9 shot for all such shooting, which in a 1/4-choke barrel should ensure decisive breaks at all distances.

Conclusions

One very important factor stands out clearly in the review of the pattern assessments in Tables 2, 3 and 4. It is the huge advantage that accrues from 'centring' the pattern right on the target. At the pattern centre, pellet strikes are 2–3 times those achieved at the periphery, and holding really 'straight' can make the difference between a 'kill' or a 'miss'. It is the ability to achieve this sort of accuracy that differentiates the top performers from those lower down the ladder. It is not surprising that the same champions are invariably very good game shots—a pheasant's head is an easier target than the front edge of a 4in saucer!

3

A History of the Sport

Chris Cradock

Chris Cradock

Clay pigeon shooting owes its origins to the book *The Art of Shooting Flying* which was first brought to England from France by the members of the court of King Charles II; from that time the shooting of moving targets, both animate and inanimate, has grown enormously. In this country the parent body for the sport, the Clay Pigeon Shooting Association, enjoys a current membership of 25,000 and there are now an estimated half a million people who shoot clays in the UK. Even in King Charles' time the art of hitting a moving object by means of another moving object was not new. King Henry VIII's archers were encouraged to practise and develop their skills by shooting at the popinjay, for which a pole thirty feet high with a six feet diameter ring at its top was fixed in the ground. Targets such as live pigeons, or even bunches of feathers, were tethered to the ring by cords; then as the ring turned, the pigeons fluttered, the bunches of feathers swung around, and the archers shot at these moving targets. In wartime the archers fired their arrows at moving human or equine targets: it must have been a nasty business to be greeted with a cloud of sharp pointed arrows, the ancient equivalent of a cloud of 'modern' pellets.

In 1785 Thomas Page wrote his book *The Art of Shooting Flying*, and his instructions for an artificial moving target set-up were as follows: two wooden poles 30 feet high to be fixed in the ground 40 yards apart, and a rope tightly strung between the pole tops; a 30in diameter wooden disc suspended from this rope by short cords fastened to two rings threaded on the rope. An 'active' man was then volunteered to run smartly away from this set-up, pulling a cord which was attached to the wooden disc; this caused the disc to slide sideways along the rope at whatever speed was generated.

Page's instructions for successfully hitting this moving target were as follows:

Give the word for the active man to start running and so moving the disc along the rope. As soon as you see it move, cock your gun and present it at the mark. As soon as you see the muzzles just before it, briskly draw the trigger, but continue in the same motion for some time after in case the gun hang fire, or not fire as quick as it ought to.

Page was thus one of the first to advise 'maintained lead'. For those not conversant with flintlocks, the reasons for his advice are these: to fire a flintlock, the trigger had first to be pulled to release the cock; this cock was actually a flintlock vice driven by a spring. When released, this flint struck the combined steel and pan cover; this moved the cover from over the pan which contained the priming powder, and as the edge of the flint slid down the surface of the steel, the resulting shower of sparks ignited the powder in the pan. All then being well, this ignited powder eventually ignited the charge of powder in the chamber of the gun barrel!

The quality of the powder in the pan, and the strength and size of the shower of sparks from the flint, all had a bearing on the speed with which the main powder charge was ignited and the gun fired. This variance of ignition time made it essential for the shooter to keep swinging his gun with a maintained lead in front of a crossing target until his gun eventually fired.

Experiments were conducted to ascertain the total average time taken, from the moment the trigger was pulled, for the cock to release, the powder in the pan to ignite and the main powder charge in the chamber to ignite until finally the pellets impinged on a 40-yard target: a total time of 0.2329 of a second was established. A modern percussion capped cartridge when fired requires a total time of only 0.1481 of a second from hammer release to pellets hitting a 40-yard target. This means that the pellets from a modern cartridge get there in about half the elapsed time of the pellets fired from a flintlock gun.

Once the art of shooting flying had been invented there was a rapid development in most shooters' skills. Soon, live moving targets were being used for practice by sportsmen wishing to become proficient in this new art. A sparrow, starling or pigeon would be placed on the ground and covered by the shooter's top hat; the shooter would then pick up his hat (covering the live bird) and quickly put it on his head—as the bird then quite naturally flew away, the shooter had to quickly mount and fire his gun at its retreating tail. This led to practitioners of the new art forming Top Hat Clubs.

This form of shooting was soon too slow for some shooters, so a man who became known as a trapper was detailed to stand behind a wall or in a ditch and throw single live birds into the air as and when the shooter called. Alternatively a single bird was placed in each of a row of five collapsible boxes or traps. The shooter stood at a set yardage from these traps, and the trapper would release one pigeon at random from any trap when a shooter called. Much money was wagered on these live pigeon contests.

When Col Hawker wrote his book *Instructions to Young Sportsmen* in the early 1800s, he too pressed into his service an active man to throw potatoes, small turnips and suchlike into the air so he could shoot his fowling piece in the practice of the art of shooting flying. The Colonel also lived to see the introduction of the percussion cap, which was an improvement over the flintlock due to quicker, more certain ignition.

There were arguments on the merits of various barrel lengths, as today. Moreover shooters could challenge the weight of the shot load in a competitor's gun. Again, as today, there were disagreements on the interpretation of the

Live pigeon from traps, 1880

gun-down position: some shooters tended to creep when calling for targets. In truth, humans change but little, and these problems are still with us . . . .

By the 1880s game, rabbit and wildfowl shooting had become very popular amongst the landed gentry in their large estates. Many thousands of pheasants and partridges were reared and when they were sufficiently mature, they were driven over strategically positioned lines of shooters. The sport expanded, some sportsmen shooting six days a week through the season. In 1890 King Edward VII described a day's shooting in the course of which his party shot 2,600 rabbits and 408 pheasants. During another very busy two days' shooting the royal party of ten guns shot 7,843 head of pheasants and rabbits.

Inevitably, the growth of the British shooting school had a great deal of influence on clay target shooting; some British gunmakers had set up their own shooting schools well before 1900—Holland and Holland's famous school, still in business, was established in 1835. With such large-scale expansion of game rearing and game shooting on the big estates at that time, it was natural that many game shooters began using British shooting schools as a means to improve their subsequent performances when shooting live game. These shooting schools could produce a well fitted gun for any of their clients. They did this by means of the try gun and pattern plates, plus expert coaching in conjunction with released sparrows, starlings, blue rock pigeons and so on. Equally important, their coaches could teach anyone with normal physical strength and co-ordination how best to tackle these moving targets. In short, the British gun trade plus their shooting school staff had the know-how to make guns and to fit them, plus the proven ability to teach their clients to shoot safely and well.

The American (left) and the English (right) 'gun down' positions

The expert teaching provided at these schools resulted in the rapid development of the shooting skills of their clients; this in turn led to the establishment of more schools. As a result, all the successful schools were very soon desperately looking for inanimate targets to throw as a substitute for the live bird targets they had been using. Many weird inanimate objects such as glass balls, wooden blocks, wooden darts and spinning propellers were tried and found wanting. Eventually, around 1880, an American called George Ligowsky designed his clay pigeon target: this was disc-shaped, made of baked clay, and aerodynamically stable when thrown, spinning, from the arm of a clay trap; it proved to be an ideal inanimate target for the shooting schools. When these targets first became available, British schools used them as well as live birds for instruction and practice; in the 1880s Charles Lancaster offered clients at his London school a choice of clay

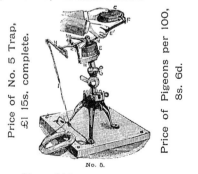

The Lancaster School in 1890

targets or live pheasants projected from his high tower. Thus clients could practise on inanimate or live targets to improve their skills.

In 1887 the famous American exhibition shooter Annie Oakley visited London with Buffalo Bill and his Wild West Show. Annie went to Lancaster's school for lessons, and eventually Lancaster made her pairs of fitted 12- and 20-bore guns. Subsequently Annie wrote and thanked Lancaster for the guns and the lessons, asserting that 'since using your guns and receiving a few lessons shooting clays at your splendid private shooting grounds, my shooting has much improved'.

In 1896 Payne Gallwey wrote an illustrated article for *Badminton* magazine entitled 'A visit to a modern shooting school' in which he described

The Holland & Holland School, 1896

39

various layouts and traps at Holland & Holland's famous school. The illustrations showed a fine pavilion, pattern plates, clay pigeons thrown over a fence like driven partridge, clays sent over trees like driven pheasants, and targets for gunfitting. There were also disappearing and re-appearing silhouette pigeons and pheasants, try guns, a tower—in short, the lot! There was everything the sportsman required to assure himself of a superbly fitted gun and expert shooting of live quarry.

British gunmakers were producing their ideal game gun before the turn of the century. At first these were 12-bore side-by-side hammerless ejectors, beautifully designed and impeccably made; the materials and craftsmanship were the finest available. Many of these guns digested thousands of cartridges without trouble, and in fact there are many such guns made a century ago which are still as sound and tight as the day they were produced. Soon after the turn of the century the over-under gun again became available, and today one can buy superb guns with side-by-side or over-under barrels which last more than one lifetime and come back for more.

Because most game was walked up or driven, in both instances a slightly high shooting gun provided its owner with a built-in lead. Therefore most game guns were, and are, stocked to throw their pattern one- to two-thirds high. This feature allowed the shooter to float crossing birds just above his gun muzzle, firing his gun whilst seeing the bird all the time. Equally important, the gun's high comb provided the owner with a far better perspective which greatly helped his gun-pointing. This perspective allowed those with normal peripheral vision to know where the muzzles were pointing in relation to the target, so cultivating 'muzzle target awareness' when the gun fired; this greatly helped clients to 'call their shots' correctly.

Although in those far-off days the shooting schools did not describe the clays they threw as 'sporting' they equated them with live birds by stating

This illustration is intended to show—Right, How an approaching high bird is to be taken. Left How the same bird would be taken behind the shooter after it has passed overhead in each instance shooting in front
No. 49]   N.B.—Face completely round and then remount. See page 99   [98

The Whymper system, 1896 – a mixture of inanimate and live targets

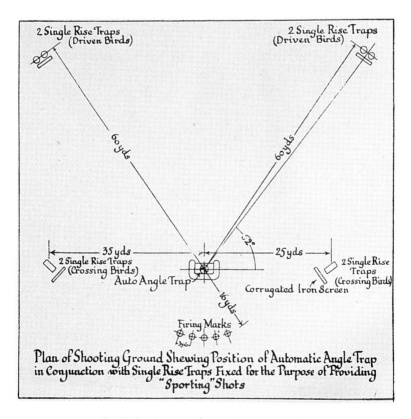

The Kelland system for sporting targets, 1925

that the trajectory of their clays simulated the flight of various game birds, describing them as 'driven partridges' or 'rocketing pheasants' flying through or over the tops of trees. In the 1880s these schools also had 'walk-ups': the shooter would move along the walk-up, and either live birds or inanimate targets were thrown 'silent rise', just as the coach wished, by remote cord control. All this was pre-1900, and proves how wrong is the modern clay pigeon shooter's belief that the shooting of sporting clay targets is a modern development, or a spin-off from English DTL or Double Rise. The illustrations by Whymper of 1896 also prove that sporting clay target shooting was very much a reality as far as the shooting schools were concerned a century ago. Thinking game and wildfowl shooters have happily visited British shooting schools for more than a hundred years to have their guns fitted, and be taught to shoot sporting clay targets *safely*.

In the 1920s when new clay clubs were installing DTL or Double Rise traps, the game shot began to press for shooting-school type sporting clays. Although at first DTL-oriented clubs designed their sporting layouts to throw mostly DTL type targets, in 1925 the Kelland Gun Club designed their ideal sporting layout, 'an auto trap in conjunction with eight single rise traps for the purpose of providing sporting shots'. These included targets going away, or towards the shooter, and also dropping in front.

An advertisement for the first Sporting Championship, 1925

**Northampton Shooting Ground, an excellent facility catering for all the
principal clay shooting disciplines**

The sport of clay shooting enjoyed more fillip when King George V went
to shoot sporting clays at West London School. Also his son Edward VIII
had clay traps fitted on the battleship *Renown* so he could practise clay
shooting on his travels to the Colonies.

The first British Sporting Clay Championship was shot in 1925. Most
targets were then thrown as going away, although clay clubs with DTL or
Double Rise appreciated the demand from game shooters to throw sporting
clay targets as practice for the real thing. In fact these game shots discovered what the shooting schools had long advocated—that good coaching
plus practice shooting at clay targets greatly improved anyone's subsequent
game-shooting performance. The established DTL clay shooter also soon
discovered that shooting sporting clays was great fun and a tremendous
challenge. Not surprisingly they also found that practice and coaching
enabled them to become more efficient and better performers when shooting sporting competitions, as a result, these specialist DTL clubs set up
stands for the practice shooting of sporting clays similar to those shot at
shooting schools or at clubs with special sporting layouts. The result?
Modern sporting targets are *not* adapted DTL targets but are sporting
targets thrown high, wide and handsome, FITASC (or international)
sporting clays competitions being the pinnacle as far as sporting targets are
concerned.

Increasingly, live quarry shooters realised that the shooting of sporting
clay targets helped their subsequent game shooting. The influence of British
shooting schools soon led to a more realistic type of sporting clay target

being thrown, even at the previously mainly DTL clubs. Rough shooters and wildfowlers also realised how shooting these sporting clays improved their performances when shooting the real thing, so they too joined clay clubs where they could shoot the more challenging shooting-school type of sporting clays.

Another factor is unchanged: DTL and other going-away disciplines are not too difficult for Mr Average to be taught to shoot twenty-five straights—but to get right to the top is as difficult as ever, and to remain there for any time is more so. The competition to succeed in any clay discipline is now so fierce that it requires 100 per cent concentration and performance on the part of the winner. A little luck may also sometimes help.

Let us consider the development of the modern clay target. In the early days there was only the standard (110mm) target; an attempt to introduce a smaller target called the midget, was made pre-war, but it did not catch on. Now we have the 90mm or midi-target, the rabbit, the battue, and the mini (60mm) target which has been described as a demented aspirin! In the 1920s, 60 yards was about the maximum distance for most targets; now, in 1992, some targets are being thrown double that distance—yet the improved performance of modern cartridges means these targets are being consistently killed. Even more spectacular are those targets loaded with coloured powder, which one used in the shoot-offs for international trap and skeet disciplines.

To sum up, modern clay targets are the fruitful outcome of a century of development, much of this a result of work done by British gunmakers in conjunction with the fine shooting schools they have established. Holland & Holland still operate their shooting school at Ducks Hill, Northwood in London, and there are many other schools which have been operating with success for years. There are hundreds of successful clubs affiliated to the governing body cf the sport, the Clay Pigeon Shooting Association (CPSA), most of these clubs have their own safety officers and CPSA coaches. Note that paid-up members are covered for up to £2 million third party insurance; it therefore makes good sense for any would-be clay shooter to become a CPSA member, then to choose and join any local clay club affiliated to the association. The club's safety officer and/or coach will be ready and willing to help.

PART 2
THE DISCIPLINES

4
Sporting Techniques

Introduction
Mike Barnes

It is a simple fact that in order to hit a moving target it is essential to aim at where it will be, rather than where it is! In other words, if you shoot *at* it, then you will miss. The distance in front of the target at which the shot will be taken is known as forward allowance or 'lead', and this is all part and parcel of the appeal of clay pigeon shooting—the enormous thrill and satisfaction of breaking long-range targets by having the courage to give the proverbial 'five-bar gate' in terms of lead.

Fair enough, but how does any shooter know how much lead to give a 60mph crossing target at 25 yards? There is plenty of statistical information available, but this is surely rendered useless when in situ as there is no time for cross-reference. The answer lies in technique, since a perfected technique will instinctively compel the shooter to make the correct decision. There are three principal methods of shooting:

1 CPSA method
2 Maintained lead
3 Swing-through

Swing-through is based on the old Churchill method where the gun is raised on the target, mounted, swung through and shot all in one. It is good for certain types of targets, and was great no doubt on driven game of modest height and for those with exceptional hand/eye co-ordination. But as a basis for clay pigeon shooting it can be discounted because it is too dependent on the temperament and instincts of the individual.

For clays, a totally dependable technique is necessary, regardless of the type of target or the mood of the individual. People talk of biorhythms in sport, and there is no question but that for some unaccountable reason you perform better on some days than others. It could be something you have eaten or drunk, the amount of sleep you have or haven't had. There are days when you arrive at the shoot brimming with confidence but when it comes to pulling the trigger, the targets keep slipping away from you—it is impossible to put your finger on it.

So what is needed is a sound technique which even on those off-days can be

Opposite
Bill Hammond (CPSA coach) at Bisley's Cottesloe Heath

relied upon to carry you through and to keep your score at a respectable level.

The CPSA method has been proved and tested by thousands of shooters over the years. It is based on the simple premise of coming up from behind the target, then tracking briefly before pulling through and squeezing the trigger at an optimum point in front—but without ever stopping the swing. Your brain in this instance is your computer, which as a result of watching the target closely and tracking it, will intuitively dictate the amount of lead necessary to break it.

Roger Silcox and Mike Reynolds both teach styles based upon this method. They differ slightly inasmuch as Roger tends to mount onto or into the bird and then pulls through, while Mike makes a deliberate point of coming up from behind, and tends to track the bird a little more than Roger. However, the principle is the same, and they are both excellent coaches who get results.

The maintained-lead method is explained in Robin Scott's chapter. 'Move, Mount, Shoot' is the name given to a variation of maintained lead devised and used by former World Sporting Champion John Bidwell. Conventional maintained lead is universally adopted by top American skeet shooters, who achieve staggering levels of success with it. See also Ed Scherer's chapter on English skeet (see p. 99). In this concept, the gun is mounted to where the target will be without going through the process of 'picking it up', but basically tracking in front; it is based on the notion that the brain has a capacity to read the situation—just as when a ball is thrown at a moving object, the thrower will automatically know where to aim the ball.

There is also a chapter—'Positive Shooting', by Mike Yardley—which deals solely with the shooter who concentrates purely on the target, to the exclusion of all else. It is a derivation of the CPSA method, in which the shooter induces a kind of radar effect into his shooting. I remember Joe Neville, an outstanding shot and coach, once telling me to read 'CCI' on the clay; in other words, to concentrate on the clay so strongly that I could read the manufacturer's name on it—the clay takes over from everything. It works!

Indeed all methods work, but to make the most progress you must choose one and stick with it. When it is perfected you can experiment, but *not until* that time; while our top sporting shooters each have a favoured method, a style which works for them, for certain targets they might use something different.

A depth of experience can count in this respect. As another former World Champion Barry Simpson once told me, all sporting targets can be likened to a series of memories. While all layouts are different, each borrows something from somewhere else. It is very possible that at some point you have shot that target before—once that is acknowledged, a plan of attack can be implemented. This could mean a couple of further extra targets in a competition, the difference between winning and being an also-ran.

I would not suggest for a minute that mastery of *all* styles is essential for anyone to progress, far from it. For most of us, mastery of the basics of the CPSA method will probably offer quickest and soundest early progress; preparation and gun-mount are the keys to good and successful shooting, and a clear understanding of what needs to be done in order to effect a clean kill of the target.

FITASC sporting . . . and shaping up to a fast, low target. The variety of sporting birds which can be presented is endless

Turning for a bird from the left – the shooter will use footwork for the on-report target from the low tower

Right: Tricky . . . a pair of curling battues. When shooting, the competitor should forget about others waiting their turn behind him

Pausing to clear the barrels is one method of keeping cool and stopping yourself rushing the targets

If I can pass on anything that I have learned over and above the content of the following chapters, it is to do as you are told! I 'muddled through' for far too long believing that in time, all would fall into place—perhaps this blind belief that it would come right was based on my knowing that I have an average-to-decent eye; but I do regret not having had a series of lessons, and not listening more readily to those who could have helped.

I think the problem often arises due to the fact that it is possible in clay shooting to make some good early progress. An early upward spiral in scores seems to indicate that you are making waves in the right direction. But in actual fact what happens is that after a while the progress comes to a bit of a halt, and you hit one of two plateaux: 50–60 or 60–70 per cent. Some days you go below, on others you rise above it and feel you are back on the rails again. However, the good scores can easily delude anyone into believing that the bad scores are merely off-days; a cold analysis of the overall level of performance will reveal that your shooting has in fact stopped going forward.

In my own instance, my particular plateau is undoubtedly due to the fact that I never mastered a sound technique. I am working at it, though I know now that if I had got off to the right footing in the early days and resisted the headstrong notion that 'I knew best', then my progress would have continued and I wouldn't have hit the Seventy Barrier.

I suppose there are three factors which hold us back from taking lessons: (i) cost; (ii) a belief that with practice you will improve, and (iii) that initially scores often drop.

There are three simple answers: (i) a relatively small outlay might save years of frustration; (ii) bad practice will harm your shooting; (iii) once under the wing of a coach, the amendments to style and technique *can* detract from the task of breaking clays—until the old habits have been kicked into touch, the scores *can* be (temporarily) reluctant to rise. However, once they do, they quickly push past Seventy into complete respectability.

With clay shooting there is compensation for us stubborn learners and slow developers: the wonderful thing about the sport is that it is never too late, and having recognized your own faults, there is then the pleasure of anticipating better times to come. And next time out will be different. Indeed it might be!

The Disciplines

Before considering the methods of clay shooting in more detail, it is perhaps worth discussing briefly the sport's different disciplines.

Sporting shooting

By far the most popular form of shooting is sporting: this is based on the simulation of live sporting quarry such as driven pheasant, crossing pigeon, springing teal, bolting rabbit and so on. Part of the reason for its popularity is its sheer variety, in that each shooter will face a different course every time he goes out to shoot, a new challenge on every outing. The other reason for its popularity is that gun clubs do not have to build permanent layouts, thus avoiding both expense and longer-term worries about planning regulations.

Sporting is also good inasmuch as it can be as easy or as difficult as an organiser wishes to make it; a round of thirty or fifty targets can present the competitor with a whole variety of challenges. By learning shooting through sporting, the individual will therefore develop a basic all-round understanding of the sport.

Those who excel in sporting will probably progress to FITASC (or international) sporting, where shoot organisers go to great lengths to make each target different from the last, and guns shoot in squads of six to recapture the atmosphere of being in the field. However, it is complicated to stage, and there is a limit as to the number of competitors that can be accommodated. Nonetheless this is the ultimate challenge for the sporting shooter, and is the discipline at which our top sporting shooters compete at international level.

The formal layout disciplines of clay pigeon shooting fall into two categories: skeet and trap.

Skeet

There are essentially two forms of skeet in this country: English skeet and ISU Olympic skeet; English is the easier of the two, and by far the most popular. In both there are two traps situated at opposite ends of a 'D'-shaped layout; a round of twenty-five English will be shot from seven points on the arc of the D, while for ISU there is also a station 8 at a midway point between the two houses.

The sequence of targets differs between the two, and there are three further essential differences:

1 English skeet targets are slower
2 It is permissible to shoot English skeet gun-up, *ie* with gun pre-mounted
3 There is a delay of up to 3 seconds on Olympic, so that the target does not necessarily appear instantly upon calling for it.

Olympic skeet is very challenging and offers the individual the opportunity of representing Great Britain in World Championships and the Olympic Games, where it is one of only two clay sports included in the programme.

On the other hand for the beginner, English skeet is a very useful way of cutting teeth: first, on a round of twenty-five there will be every kind of target, from driven and going away, to quartering and crossing. It encourages good gun-mounting and smooth swing; also, it will be possible to build confidence with good progress, and to improve overall ability.

Probably the most significant factor about skeet is that it highlights the importance of concentration, something which also makes it such a fascinating competitive discipline. The top performers know they can break every target on a round, but the holding together of a hundred targets calls for steely nerve and strong resolve.

There is yet one other form of skeet shooting in the UK: on the shooting ranges of Britain's American air bases, NSSA skeet (the American equivalent of English) is popular.

Trap shooting

When it comes to trap shooting there are endless permutations, but basically they all consist of angling going-away targets thrown from a trap which is positioned in front of a line of five or six shooters; these take it in turns to shoot from five different positions on the line behind the trap. Hence the name 'Down the Line' derives from the act of moving down the line to take shots from the different pegs. It is the most popular of the trap disciplines. It is also the easiest, since targets travel at only modest speeds to fairly limited angles. But again, like skeet, it is a tremendously useful discipline on which to learn, for it really does instil the importance of total concentration—no target is in the bag until it is shot.

There are variants on DTL such as Single Barrel, Handicap by Distance, Double Rise and American Trap. Then there are the more sophisticated trap disciplines, starting with Automatic Ball Trap, moving through Universal Trap to the ultimate game of this sort, Olympic trap with its fifteen traps (three in front of each shooting peg) throwing targets at fast and widely varying angles. This, and the new Double Trap, are the disciplines which enjoy Olympic status. Olympic trap is recognised as the cream of the trap sports.

A variant on trap is ZZ, which has a limited but growing following; it is explained by Pat Lynch later in the book (see p. 140).

The chapter on techniques aims to give a comprehensive understanding of the basics of good clay pigeon shooting. Once mastered, the shooter can make his choice on preferred disciplines—I admit to a preference for sporting, but thoroughly enjoy a round of skeet, either English or Olympic, and though I don't often get the chance to shoot trap, a couple of rounds always leaves me wanting to take it up more seriously. I'm a great fan of all-round shooting—competitions which include all three of the principal disciplines.

Better Shooting

Mike Reynolds

Shooting, like most things in life, is best done simply. It is always easy to become technical, use jargon that sounds impressive, quote statistics and logistics that would confound even the most knowledgeable layman, but at the end of the day much of this merely clouds the issue of learning how to become a good shot. It is the basics which matter, and the important ingredients of good shooting are these:

• Gun-fit
• Gun-mounting
• Balance
• Footwork
• Approach

If you notice, none of these actually mentions pulling the trigger! The reason for this is that the essence of good shooting lies in the groundwork: if the correct procedure is followed, taking the shot comes naturally.

Gun-fit cannot be underestimated. The top shot will be able to shoot well with most things, but the beginner or novice will find it impossible if he cannot mount the gun properly. The better-known makes of modern sporting shotguns are all built to a very good standard nowadays, yet the respective brand names have different ideas on stock dimension. The comb height on a Browning and a Beretta will be different, and then we in turn are all built differently. So how can we expect any gun to be of a perfect fit?

The importance is often emphasised by people who visit my ground. We have a father and daughter who are regulars, and recently 'mother' decided to take up the sport. She shot gun-up, with a gun that was too short, didn't fit and kicked her every time she pulled the trigger. How could she possibly have expected to shoot with such a gun? In fact she had actually been told that she needed a short stock because she was a woman! I put a one-inch pad on the stock, adjusted the comb, and she is now shooting gun-down and extremely well.

Another club member treated himself to a lovely Browning B2G. It had a beautiful piece of wood and he showed it to me proudly. I put it to my shoulder and knew straightaway that even allowing for the differences in our build, it needed altering—on mounting the gun, all I could see was the top lever.

'There is no way that I am altering a beautiful gun like this,' he told me. He clearly wasn't going to be swayed, so I let him get on with it.

A few weeks later I happened to be near the skeet layout while he was in action. He missed several targets, and it was obvious that he was missing them all underneath. He is actually quite a good shot, and not being slow to enjoy a bit of Mickey-taking, I congratulated him on his performance. He said that he could not understand why he had hit such a rough patch. So I

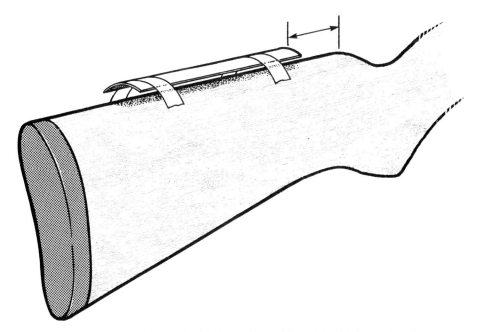

Simple DIY gun fitting: build the stock up with card (or thick paper) and
sticky tape. Keep going until you think the height is right, then ask your local
gunsmith to bend it to the required height

suggested that he borrow a friend's gun, an almost identical B2G—he
looked at me a bit sideways, but took the gun to station 4 and centred the
targets perfectly. However, he was just as bewildered as when he had been
missing them. 'The gun's just the same as mine,' he said. 'In every respect
but the comb height,' I told him. The penny dropped, he had the gun
altered, and he was back on full song in no time.

I mention these two instances as examples of how both novice and quite
experienced shooters can handicap themselves by using good guns which
do not fit them. Any shooting school will be able to advise on gun-fit, but
those who do not have a school nearby can easily to a little DIY gun-fitting;
all you need is some cardboard and sticky tape. Build up the comb with
card until you feel that you get the correct sight picture when you mount—
that is, just a little of the barrel rib showing. It is a good idea to shoot with
the gun a few times until you feel that you have got it right, then visit a
local gunsmith who will be able to take down your measurements. Bending
a stock to fit is a relatively simple job for a gunsmith and will cost relatively
little.

Obviously, a gun that doesn't fit will not permit the user to mount it in
the same place every time; it is therefore impossible to reach any level of
consistency with such a gun. Given a good fit, I like to teach people to shoot
with their body moving into the target; with the weight on the leading front
foot, the shooter is then permitted to take maximum advantage of his
natural instinct.

Shooting driven, using the classic English front foot method.
Note that almost all the weight is on the leading leg

No-one can teach a club shooter how to become a top shot overnight, but it is nonetheless perfectly possible for most to climb away from the 40–50 per cent mark which is such a hurdle in the early stages. With a bit of method and thinking, a very fair percentage of average shooters should be capable of hitting 70–75 per cent of sensible sporting targets. The only reason why people find it difficult to progress to this level is through not having a total grasp of what they are actually doing. They simply copy others blindly, rather than perfecting a method which can be relied upon; their shooting becomes a patchwork. Yet broken down, the step-by-step stages to good shooting are really quite simple.

It is often interesting to study closely the performance of our top shots. I was on the same squad as Barry Simpson in a European Sporting Championship; Barry is a very good shot, one of our best, but his style appears quite different to my own. Yet close scrutiny will reveal that in fact while Barry's actual stance is different to mine, he nevertheless goes through all the procedures which I recommend to my pupils. He positions himself perfectly, addresses the target, picks it up and tracks it over the muzzles before shooting. Finally he takes the shot quickly in one flowing motion; but this is no more than a procedure which has been finely tuned and speeded up through experience. Otherwise he depends totally on flawless approach work—and this is what I like to get across to my pupils. Do the simple things well, and the shooting becomes easy.

Adrenalin

There is another part of the equation which is most important to successful shooting, but about which very little has been written. It's called adrenalin, and there's another word for it—panic! It can arise at any point in a shoot, and is sure to show itself when shooting simultaneous pairs. How often when watching a stand of pairs will you see at least one of the shots being rushed, maybe both? The cause will almost certainly be the feeling of pressure to which the individual in question subjects himself.

The highlight of a shooter's year might be a big event at the local club, it might be a major national CPSA championship; these are occasions which are looked forward to enormously, but unfortunately as a result the individual can become extremely keyed up about the whole thing. The anticipation might become so great that come the day of the event he might find it almost impossible to keep his nerves under control. The adrenalin will be flowing, and while its effects if channelled properly can be hugely beneficial, for most it will in fact thoroughly impair their performance. Timing becomes stiff, a flinch might appear and then there is a loss of co-ordination; confidence simply drains away.

This is a worrying state of affairs, but it is a condition which affects most of us at some time or another. The top shooters will be able to turn adrenalin to their advantage because of their greater experience and confidence—they know they can break targets because they have done the same or similar so many times before. The adrenalin will instead sharpen their senses and they will become utterly ruthless about the task in hand.

So, what about us ordinary mortals? My answer is that the same applies: everyone knows his own capabilities and it is important to be honest with yourself in this respect. You have broken targets at a local club so you know you can do it, and the clay targets used in major championship are no different to any other: they are there to be broken.

Having arrived at the ground you will have booked in, and probably had a coffee and a chat. When you feel ready, find yourself a straightforward stand to start on. It is not always a good idea to spend a long time walking the course beforehand. It can work against you, especially if you let a difficult stand prey on your mind—you will think about that one and not much else, and as a result you make a mess of the easy stands.

The really important part of it all is to approach each stand with the utmost confidence. You know you can do it, so stay relaxed and think about what you are going to do. Forget all that is going on around you—nothing else matters but you and the target. Don't listen to others, or copy someone who just happens to get a good score on a particular stand—his style may be totally different to yours. Besides, he may have hit a rare purple patch. Just stick to your guns and do what you know best.

Again, it's all relatively simple and depends largely on the basics. Instead of worrying, watch the targets as others shoot and make a mental note of some kind of landmark—a twig, a leaf or piece of earth—at which they come into view. You will then pick up the line of the clay at the earliest possible point and there will be no need to rush. You will be able to select a position which will enable you to take the shot at its easiest.

Never hurry the target. If it's a simultaneous pair, remember that the birds will be much slower than a single; the trap will not be capable of throwing a fast pair. If it's a pair on report, give yourself plenty of time for the first bird and be standing in a position that will enable you to move easily onto the second. As the second will not be released until you have fired, use that time to your advantage.

Never fall out with referees. If you think that you have been given a loss when you hit the bird, ask *politely* if he was sure. If he insists it was a loss, accept his decision gracefully—it's only one target. So often shooters

That's smoking! Build confidence with more straightforward targets

become highly agitated in this sort of situation, and consequently throw away a fistful of targets. Remember the referee is there to help you and will be doing his job to the best of his ability, so *do not* get angry. If you reach a point where by the eighth stand you have put a decent score together (even if only by your own standards) don't let the pressure get to you. Nor is it advisable to take a coffee break, as you could lose your rhythm. Just take a deep breath, relax and let the confidence return; put your trust in the basics and they will see you through.

Similarly, try not to become despondent about shooting a stand badly. At sporting you can come back. There is only one winner in any class, but it's a lot better to come second than last; and even better still to produce a score which is a personal best. It's an occasion you have looked forward to, so make the most of it.

Problem Target

Move the gun from behind the clay, track it, then push through it on
the flight line and shoot

Finally, what about bad patches? We all have them, and shooting is no different to any other sport in this respect. And like any other sport, the answer is to go back to the basics. Are you doing everything correctly? How is your stance and gun-mount, and are you lifting your head? Check and double check. If things don't improve, speak to someone about your problem—a good shooting school will soon put you back on the right track.

Even if you feel that you are doing everything properly, there may still be a problem target which is causing concern; the most common of these is without doubt the left-to-right crosser. (Unless of course the out-of-touch shot is a left-hander, in which case it will be the right-to-left crosser.) Speak to any number of people, and you will be given different theories as to why this should be such a source of irritation for so many. And particularly if it's a constant source of irritation, in which one would tend to think that with enough practice it would be possible to correct the fault.

Some say that the gun swings more slowly from left to right, others feel it is due to the stopping of the gun; there is also a sound argument for the right-hander having a natural swing across the body, just like a boxer. It has been suggested that with the swing from the right, the stock is moving into

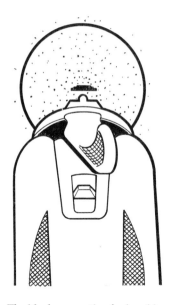

The ideal perspective for breaking the clay – by seeing just a little of the rib you will be able to keep the target in view while you shoot

the face and therefore it is much easier to maintain a correct mount; move it the other way, and it can lift off the cheek.

One thing is for sure, left-to-right crossers are much more of a problem for right-handed shots that any other targets, so don't feel that you have an isolated and incurable disease! Equally you should ignore all of the above, because the *real* reason why this type of target can prove such a problem is that it is an optical illusion!

All accurate shooting depends ultimately on sight picture and hand/eye co-ordination. If that picture is misleading, then the co-ordination is much less likely to bring about the appropriate movement and timing necessary to kill the target. Think about it. If a bird is moving from right to left, after you have mounted and tracked the target, you will swing through as it crosses in front of you: your gun will therefore be moving across your face between your vision and the clay.

What actually happens is that you are giving more lead than you realise, due to part of the lead being obscured by the barrels of your gun. Remember that inches at the barrel equate to feet at 20–30 yards. Conversely, on a left-to-right crosser, the gun moves away from the target and the eye has a perfect picture of the amount of lead given. The distance looks the same as for the right-hander—but isn't!

Left-to-right crosser: look for the bird with the gun ready to 'pick it up'

Get onto it, then move in front and shoot

In other words, because of the misleading picture on the right-to-left, you have in fact given more forward allowance than you realised. On the left-to-right you have given exactly the amount you wish, but this is almost certainly not enough! Consequently people will hit right-to-lefts, yet claim that given a target of the same distance and speed but travelling in the opposite direction they will regularly miss. They think they are giving the same lead to both targets, but they are not.

It is a fact that due to speed of swing and sight picture, no two people will give the same amount of forward allowance for a target. As an example, if someone shoots a 25-yard crosser he may estimate that as a right-to-left target he has given it three feet allowance—in fact he is most likely to have given it five feet. When he gives it three feet in the opposite direction he will miss.

You can double-check the theory quite simply. The next time you shoot a left-to-right crosser, as you are about to pull the trigger push the barrels a little further and see what happens. You must at all times, however, remember to apply the basics: good stance, weight distribution and good gun-mounting. When it is your turn to shoot a crosser, stand in the shooting position, first and foremost facing the point at which you expect to take the target. Notice that when top shots are waiting their turn, they will not only very carefully study the flight of the target, and from what point they can actually see it, they will also decide exactly where they will kill the bird and how they will stand in order to do so.

Stand facing the point where you expect to shoot the target; then turn to look for it as it comes into view. In effect from that moment you unwind like a coiled spring, so that by the time you have watched it over the barrel muzzles, mounted, tracked and pulled through, the tension has totally gone from your body and you are completely free to take the shot. As long as your stance and gun-mount are sound, then the theories about the gun coming off the cheek and against the natural swing hold little water.

It's just a simple case of not being what it appears.

Mike Reynolds is the proprietor of Mid-Norfolk Shooting School, near Norwich, where he has successfully coached many top shooters as well as run some of the most successful sporting competitions ever held in this country, including six British Open Sporting Championships.

Remember to think where the target will be, rather than where it is

The CPSA Method

Roger Silcox

Imagine you are faced with a relentless, merciless enemy that you have to destroy at all costs. You have only one short-range weapon at your disposal and only one or, at best, two rounds of ammunition left. Your enemy, however, has two big disadvantages—he is defenceless and predictable.

With prior planning and good strategy you *should* emerge victorious every time. By now you will have realised that I am describing the shooting of a clay target and not a battle . . . but it is a battle!

To shoot well requires more than technique, expertise and the right equipment. You need a plan of attack. Your first move has to be an intelligence-gathering operation, conducted from the best vantage point possible. Merely looking at the target as it sails through the air is useless—the referee and spectators have been doing this for hours and are in no better position to kill the target than you are.

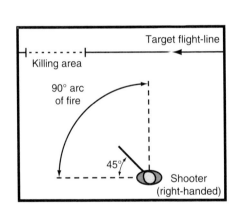

Target flight-line

Killing area

90° arc
of fire

45°

Shooter
(right-handed)

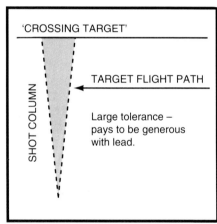

'CROSSING TARGET'

TARGET FLIGHT PATH

SHOT COLUMN

Large tolerance –
pays to be generous
with lead.

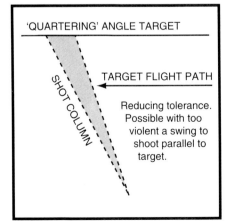

'QUARTERING' ANGLE TARGET

TARGET FLIGHT PATH

SHOT COLUMN

Reducing tolerance.
Possible with too
violent a swing to
shoot parallel to
target.

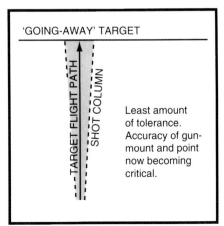

'GOING-AWAY' TARGET

TARGET FLIGHT PATH

SHOT COLUMN

Least amount
of tolerance.
Accuracy of gun-
mount and point
now becoming
critical.

Picking the observation point is of prime importance: the only place from which you can make a completely accurate assessment of the target's flight-line is from the shooting stand. In an ideal situation that is what you should do.

If this is not possible, try to stand at such an angle (safety and consideration for others permitting) that the only factor which will alter when you walk forward to shoot is the distance to the target. Failure to appreciate this fundamental is the cause of many lost targets, particularly the first shot on the stand. I have frequently observed, and experienced, the surprise of finding that the flight angle, target 'pick-up point' and trajectory are different from that originally anticipated.

Having picked your observation point, the next priority is to assess the target accurately. From where does it appear—out of a trap-house, from behind a tree or above a hedge? More specifically, does it appear in line with a particular branch on a tree or the centre of the trap-house? Is the background such that it can be seen easily?

Visual contact having been established, you must continue your assessment of the flight-line by noting its vertical and horizontal path, the influence of wind, change of background (and thus its visibility) and its speed. The most important part of this flight-line is 'the killing or engagement area'.

Target trajectory and speed are never constant, and are therefore also changing constantly relative to the shooter. Failure to appreciate this is also the cause of many missed targets. My own teacher always emphasised the importance of 'reading the target'.

Your movement has to be as smooth and controlled as possible—it must be sympathetic to, or 'mirror' the target flight as it is relative to you. For example, an incoming target coming from a distance will have a slow movement initially which accelerates as it approaches, even though it is itself physically slowing.

You must therefore start with a slow movement that accelerates as the target approaches, your movement being continually amended as you update your assessment of the target.

The opposite is the case with a going-away target, as your ability to make accurate assessments diminishes rapidly as it gets further away. The target, which initially appeared to be climbing fast and going straight, may well be dropping and curling as it loses velocity.

As already said, assessment of target behaviour in the anticipated 'killing area' is extremely important and, of course, may well influence the selection of the ideal killing area. The 'springing teal' is a prime example of the foregoing.

As always, what goes up must come down, and many a target of this type is missed 'over the top' because it was already responding to the force of gravity as the shot was fired. Incidentally, where possible it is much easier to assess this type of target from the side than from behind; it needs careful planning as it is deceiving—initial impressions are usually false.

By contrast, a wide crosser is far easier to read as its change of angle and speed relative to the shooter is slow. A small movement on your part is a relatively large one for the target at, say, 40 yards.

65

So, where the 'going-away' target may need to be shot quickly while it is still behaving as initially assessed, the wide crosser can be dealt with more steadily because the angles change more slowly and the movement of the target is also relatively slow.

A good way to appreciate these points is to extend an arm and forefinger and track a target across the sky. Removing the stress of trying to kill the target will make it much easier for your 'computer' to assess it. Many top class performers do this. Always use your 'front arm' (left arm if you shoot from the right shoulder), and pick the best observation point.

So, by now your computer guidance system and weapon should be fully tuned and locked on to the target by the time it reaches the killing area: the final move in the attack is, of course, destruction. By now 90 per cent of the work has been done.

At this stage it is vital that the shooter's actions become a smooth and fluent movement sympathetic with the target flight. This smoothness is probably more important at this point than at any other—suffice to say that if the gun movement is in any way erratic, then so will be the results.

The concept of lead or forward allowance is accepted by the majority of shooters. However, visualisation of lead differs considerably from person to person. Some will tell you that they shoot straight at a target to hit it, others will talk in terms of needing lead varying from inches to feet in length. Only your own experience will enable you to establish the lead (or lack of it) requirement to shoot a particular target.

Let us first consider the ballistics of the shotgun. The pellets, having left the barrel, disperse into a funnel or cone-shaped 'pattern'. Using a true cylinder barrel, the pattern spread at a range of 20 yards will be about 30–35in in diameter and at a range of 30 yards about 40–45in. In addition to this lateral spread, the pellets also spread lengthwise into a column, which at a range of 20 yards can be about 5 feet in length and 8 feet at 30 yards. This is caused by damage to the pellets as they pass along the barrel, resulting in a variation of velocity.

Notice the word 'about', as results will vary depending on the particular gun, cartridge, hardness and size of shot, and so on.

Much research has, of course, been done on the subject of shotgun ballistics and it is very easy to be too precise when trying to make lead calculations and when comparing pattern densities. Exact figures can, of course, be obtained for lead requirement with a given velocity of cartridge and a target at a given range, also shot spread and density; however, I am going to suggest that they are of academic interest only to shooters (albeit vitally important to the manufacturer).

For instance, we are told that a target crossing at a speed of 40mph at a distance of 35 yards requires a forward allowance of 6ft 8in using cartridges with a muzzle velocity of 1,070 ft per second. A 'high' muzzle velocity of 1,120 ft per second would need a lead of 6ft 5in . . . 3in difference. Well, can you judge a distance of 3in at 35 yards?

Yes, I know it is the width of a target, but this degree of precision does not have practical application . . . because shotguns are fired by people and they do vary. So, in a way we have two lead factors to consider—the technical lead, which is a constant, and the lead as visualised by you and me. We need this constant to base our lead assessment on, but the real secret of consistent shooting is developing a style or technique which is also as near constant as possible.

To recap, therefore, we are firing a 'cloud' of pellets which has length and width, and this pellet dispersion provides the tolerance that enables us to shoot with a certain consistency.

The tolerance available will, of course, vary upon the angle of flight-line relative to the shooter. When shooting a crossing target, the cloud of pellets can be likened to a wall which is going to be placed in front of the target; due to its length (8 feet at 30 yards) one can always err on the generous side when estimating lead requirement in this situation. However, as the angle between shot column and target reduces, this tolerance will also reduce, until when shooting at a straight-away target the column is providing little or no advantage at all. Therefore, when shooting going-away targets I would suggest that as open a choke as is consistent with good 'kills' should be used. In fact this is probably the best advice in all situations.

But back to the question of lead. You will probably have experienced widely different advice as to lead requirement. Why? As I have already said, we differ considerably in our visualisation of lead, our speed of reflexes, our health, our shooting methods, our stance, and even our recent diet.

The greatest variable is probably what we, as individuals, visualise in our minds as, say, a distance of 6 feet at a range of 30 yards. Stance, for instance, can influence speed of swing and thus lead requirement. A slow, deliberate movement will probably require more lead. Conversely, good health and quick reflexes may well reduce lead; an empty tummy and hungry approach could have the same effect. A poor 'follow-through' when firing will increase the need for lead.

Thus it appears that it is not possible, neither is it necessary, to give precise lead distances; what is essential is the cultivation of a method that is appropriate to the individual and which makes it possible to produce consistent and successful results. As with most things in life, with clay shooting we reap what we sow and, consequently, every part of our method and approach must be considered carefully as each part unevitably contributes to our success or failure. Consistent results will only come from an analytical assessment of our technique, enabling us to perform in the same way every time.

Let us start at ground level: foot position and stance have a considerable effect on one's ability to move and maintain balance. An excellent position for the feet is for them to be 'shoulder-width apart', a term which I think is self-explanatory; it also has the great benefit that it applies to everybody, whatever their build.

Let's experiment: hold your gun horizontally at waist level with the barrels pointing forwards (this is now your pointer). Standing with your feet as recommended, determine how far you can swing your gun from side to side in a comfortable, controlled way. Now place your feet closer together which allows more movement, maybe, but is less stable. Wider apart will allow less movement but is more stable.

Now you have to decide what suits you best. As a guide you should be able to produce a controlled 90-degree 'arc of fire' movement. While it is possible to move further than this, the ability to maintain elevation and speed deteriorates rapidly. A right-handed person will find that this 90-degree arc extends from straight ahead to a line through the left shoulder, a left-hander straight ahead to a line through the right shoulder.

When you have determined the most suitable foot position, use it every time you shoot. If you don't, you will affect your ability to move and become inconsistent.

Now, let's look at the relative angle of your feet. Most people stand naturally and comfortably with the toes slightly wider apart than the heels. Experiment as before and find out what is best. Certainly, widening the toe position usually reduces movement. Standing more or less normally, your weight will be equally distributed between your two feet; in the shooting situation, however, one normally leans forward. How much should one lean forward and how should one do it?

On average, people tend to lean forward too much, causing the 'front' shoulder to drop and the lead to lift off the gun, inhibiting the ability to move. Try this experiment:

Standing with the feet at optimum position, relax the muscles in the front leg (left leg if you are right-handed and vice versa). This will cause the knee to bend slightly and you will now find that it is possible to lift the other foot off the ground.

The object of this exercise is to show you that it is possible to bias your weight onto the front foot, relax the muscles for smooth movement and bend the front knee to give maximum movement without leaning forward in an exaggerated manner.

If this feels uncomfortable or awkward, don't do it. However, find out what *does* feel right so that you can adopt a stance which is comfortable and efficient and can be employed on all occasions. You will have too many other problems to consider when actually shooting, and no opportunity to analyse your stance then.

These experiments will almost certainly cause many people to stand with their feet closer than before. A wide stance and a pronounced lean forward are natural, aggressive attitudes but they only hinder physical movement. Planned aggression is essential, but it must be a state of mind and not something which causes muscular tension.

We must now consider the angle of the body relative to the target flight-line, which takes us back to the 90-degree arc of fire. The important part of the flight-line to consider, is the anticipated killing area, and as it is essential that the gun movement is at its optimum in this area, obviously the target must be killed within your 90-degree arc. Ideally, this would be at an angle of 45 degrees to the body.

In order to determine this position, some people advocate pointing the front toe towards the killing area. However, this is sometimes misunderstood, with the shooter simply turning the foot in order to achieve this. It should, of course, be the whole body, with the feet kept at optimum position.

One of Britain's outstanding young shots, Richard Faulds, makes good use of his time as he waits for his turn

Shooting a quartering pair from this angle they look close together, but are actually a yard apart. Never take a target for granted

Jackie Stewart was a champion clay shot before taking up motor racing, and now runs his own shooting school at Gleneagles. He is pictured here shooting at Apsley, Hampshire

You can readily determine this angle of 45 degrees by simply holding your gun naturally at approximately waist level. If you are right-handed you will find that the right arm and gun stock rest against your body and your left hand holds the barrels pointing 45 degrees to the left (left-handed people vice versa).

You are now pointing your gun towards the ideal killing position relative to the body, and simply turn body and feet so that this coincides with the ideal killing area. With a small amount of practice you will find that you can do this automatically.

If the foregoing fundamentals are understood and implemented, you will be well on the way to consistency based on thorough groundwork.

Roger Silcox (left) is the proprietor of Roses Wood Shooting Ground near Bradford-upon-Avon, Wiltshire. He is the Senior Staff Tutor of the Clay Pigeon Shooting Association, a regular contributor to Pull! *magazine, and has also produced two highly acclaimed instructional shooting videos in conjunction with Teacher's whisky.*

Positive Shooting

Michael Yardley

Safety

Always treat a gun as if it were loaded. *Never* point a gun at something you do not want to shoot.

Always check that a gun is *unloaded* when it is passed to you (or when you pass it to someone else).

When you take a gun from its slip: (a) keep your finger off the trigger, and (b) make sure the action is open before the gun is fully removed.

Never load a gun until you are in the 'cage' or designated shooting position. Before loading, check that there are no obstructions in the barrels. When you close the gun, do so with control. Never slam break-action guns shut. When you finish shooting, open the gun and make sure it is unloaded *before* leaving the shooting position. *Never turn around from your shooting position without opening and unloading your gun first..*

I have developed the Positive Shooting system to provide both novice and experienced shots with a straightforward way of improving their sporting shooting. It draws on many sources, the writings of Stanbury, Churchill and many others, the teaching methods of the Services, and not least from academic psychology. Essentially, the Positive Shooting system recognises that there are two related components of consistent shotgun marksmanship:

1 a mastery of physical technique (based on the knowledge of an effective shooting style or styles);
2 the right mental approach.

The Positive Shooting system strives to integrate physical and psychological skills. They are part of the same whole, and to consider them as anything else—as many do—invites off-days when basic technique may be sound but psychology is poor. This is a negative approach. The Positive Shooter knows that if he or she applies the integrated Positive method, the target will break. This will be discussed in more detail shortly; for now, it is enough to note that the Positive Shooter applies the same simple routine of thoughts and actions to every shot. This can be summarised as follows:

Assess the line of the target before shooting. Establish: (1) where you first see the target as a blur or streak as it exits the trap; (2) where you first see it clearly as a clay pigeon; and (3) where, approximately, you want to kill it. Set up your stance according to the chosen 'killing point'. Mount the gun (rules permitting) onto it, and wind the muzzles back along the line of flight, stopping at the point of first clear visual contact. Lower the butt from the shoulder, keeping the tip of the muzzles just under the line of flight. Now direct your eyes a little further back along the line of flight to the area where the target is first seen as a blur or streak. *Visualise the target breaking in your mind's eye.* Call for the target. As soon as you see it, start moving the gun. *Keep watching the target and nothing but the target* until it is a puff of smoke or a cluster of fragments.

The **Positive Shooting** system attempts to make the shooter more disciplined and more aware of what he or she is doing; it presents certain basic principles which are common to all good shooting with the shotgun:

Visual Contact Glue the eyes to the target and nothing but the target, from the point of first visual pick-up to the point when the target is just a puff of smoke or collection of fragments.

Balance Maintain a stance which is comfortable, stable, and which promotes a smooth, unchecked swing.

Rhythm/Timing This is hard to put into words precisely (which may be why it is so rarely considered). Essentially it is the business of shooting as if to a beat: for example, the rhythm of shooting high driven birds from the gun-down position is well expressed by the old gamekeeper's phrase YOU: ARE: DEAD. The shooter says to him or herself 'YOU' on first visual contact with the target; 'ARE' as the gun comes up to the face and shoulder; and 'DEAD' as the trigger is pulled. (When starting from the gun-down position, most sporting birds, live and artificial, are shot to three beats but the tempo changes depending on the specific type of shot. For example the tempo would slow down for a long crosser, and speed up for a close-quartering target. Think about it now: 'One, two, three', pretty snappy, on the quartering target; but 'O-n-e, T-w-o, T-h-r-e-e', on the long crosser.)

The perfect shot—which we all aspire to be—would have complete mastery of all three universals under any circumstances. Conversely, poor performance on any of the universals—though we may get away with it occasionally—means we are not shooting as well as we might. The universals may be imagined as the corners of a triangle; visual contact should be placed at the top—the focus of all one's energy—because it is the single most important thing (safety apart) in shotgun shooting.

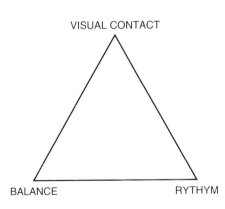

The 'universals' of shotgun marksmanship

As already noted, the Positive Shooting system presents an integrated physical and psychological system. It is based upon the fusion of a well tried basic or 'core' technique with a personal shooting ritual or programme—a means to apply consistently the basic technique and overcome the peaks and troughs of our emotional state. The ritual taught here concentrates particularly on the

73

vital preparatory stage before the shot is taken; the shooter is given a definite series of thoughts and actions with which to precede every shot. One of the most important is the positive visualisation of the kill before the shot is taken—psychologists call this 'visual rehearsal', and there is ample scientific evidence that this sort of mental activity significantly improves physical performance.

Core Technique

There are many different methods of shooting; there are different ways of standing and, most notably, there are different ways of applying forward allowance or lead to a moving target. Some advocate swinging through from behind (a.k.a. the 'smoke-trail method'); some say one should 'maintain a lead' (keep the barrels ahead of the bird from the start); and others, like the late Percy Stanbury, suggest that the tip of the gun should move with the bird initially and then accelerate in front of it as the gun comes to the face and shoulder. That is the system suggested here. However, Positive Shooting proposes (as did Robert Churchill) that on the majority of birds one should forget about consciously looking for lead, since preparation and sustained visual contact will ensure that the right amount of lead is applied to most targets automatically.

The basic mount: The 'address', or ready position

No matter what the method, a good gun-mount is the foundation stone of

good shooting; even the most experienced shots need to practise their mount regularly.

Imagine we are going to shoot at a static target immediately to our front and just above the horizon. The front foot will be at approximately 1 o'clock to the target, the rear foot at approximately 3 o'clock. The gap between the heels will be in the range of 6–8 inches; the rear heel will be slightly raised. The weight should be forward, the bulk of it on the *ball* of the front foot.

The heel of the butt will usually be held just beneath the level of the armpit, the top edge parallel with, or slightly above, the forearm (in competition, rules permitting, it may be held higher). The muzzles should be held up with the foresight bead placed just under an imaginary line from the eye to the target. The muzzles *must not* be placed above the line of the bird.

The right hand will have a comfortable but firm grip on the gun, with the web between thumb and index finger located just to the top right side of the grip, and not precisely on the top of the grip. Correct positioning of the hand ensures the minimum of tension during the mount (if the web is located on the top of the grip, mounting is awkward and there is a tendency to push the muzzles up); it also ensures that the index finger can be extended without twisting to maximise trigger control. The area on the index finger between the pad and the first joint should make contact with the trigger.

The left hand will be in a comfortable midway position on the fore-end, and not gripping too hard. The fore-end is actually held with the fingers and not rested in the palm. The left-hand index finger will be *pointing towards the target*, and will be placed along the bottom left-hand edge of the fore-end. Both elbows will be naturally positioned, pointing at about 45 degrees to the ground.

3

THE BASIC MOUNT

1 Look for the target positively, gun out of the shoulder

2 Eyes on the target over the muzzles whilst mounting

3 Into the shoulder and... another broken clay

The basic mount: Shouldering the gun

The gun stock should be raised to the face and shoulder with a co-ordinated movement of both hands. The head should remain still throughout and, though almost erect, should be very slightly tilted forward. As it comes to the face, the comb of the stock locates between the cheek and jaw-bone, which should be in firm contact with the wood but not squashed down.

A good mount involves fluid and rhythmical body movements; it is an unhurried action. During the mount, the gun will pivot about the axis of the muzzles; it will also be pushed slightly towards the target. Both hands move in concert, but the arc of movement of the rear hand is greater than that of the front. As the gun rises, the shoulder rises and should also be pushed forward slightly to meet the sole of the gun butt.

I teach my students to say 'ONE: TWO: THREE' as they mount the gun in dry practice; 'ONE' corresponds to picture 1, 'TWO' to 2, and 'THREE' to 3. I ask them to count aloud to develop their sense of rhythm, something which is not always considered in conventional shotgun instruction. You will find it very useful to practise mounting the gun at home (but do not forget *safety*, as all too many gun accidents occur at home).

The mount and swing

The basic mount involves no sideways movement of the gun. It is a useful training exercise, but in the field would only be applicable to those birds which were going away or approaching the shooter in a perfectly straight line. Most targets will require a 'swinging' motion as well. The process for a mount and swing is very like that for the basic mount, except that, after setting up the stance to the approximate killing point (which is usually the first place where the bird may be comfortably shot), the shooter must rotate back along the projected line of flight towards the point where he first sees the target clearly. This is how to kill a simple crossing target. There are two stages, *preparation* and *performance:*

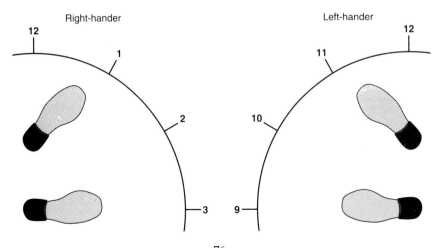

Preparation

1 Watch a few birds to see how they are flying; ask yourself if the line or speed of the bird is deceptive (it may be useful to watch others shooting).
2 Note where you first see the bird as a blur, and the point where you first see it distinctly.
3 Consider a 'killing point'—the first point where you think the bird may be shot comfortably. Do not make a final decision until you have moved into your actual shooting position.

Performance

1 Decide on your killing point and set up your stance to it—front foot at 1 o'clock, rear foot at 3 o'clock. Rules permitting, mount the gun on your intended killing point. Visualise the target being killed.
2 Keeping the gun in the shoulder (again, rules permitting), rotate back along flight-line to the point where the target is first seen distinctly.
3 Remove, or check, the safety and drop the butt from the shoulder, keeping the muzzles just under the line of flight.
4 Direct your eyes to the area where the target is first seen as a blur, and call for your target.
5 As soon as your eyes lock on to the moving clay, start the upper body and gun moving too.
6 As the gun is rising to the face and shoulder, and as the muzzles continue to move with the bird, the left hand begins to push the muzzles in front of the target.
7 The gun is fired as the butt comes firmly into the face and shoulder, and as the right lead picture is seen sub- or semi-consciously. (The shoulder will have been brought slightly forwards), and the muscles of the shoulder, neck and hands will have tensed at the moment of firing.)
8 Follow through, maintaining visual contact with the broken target.

Obviously, you will not be able to remember all of this immediately. The above list describes, fairly precisely, a sequence of actions which must be practised, not once or twice, but thousands of times before it is fully mastered. It is presented here as a reference. However, although the Positive Shooting system does not advocate that you try and commit all the preparation and performance stages to memory, *you must remember to do four things habitually every time you shoot:*

1 *Always* select the point where you first see the target clearly so you will know precisely where to point your gun while awaiting the target.
2 *Always* select a killing point and set up your stance to address it.
3 *Always* visualise what you want to achieve—a kill—before calling.
4 *Always* maintain visual contact throughout the process of shooting.

Developing your own ritual

Picture yourself now setting up your body for a crossing shot to your front, left foot at 1 o'clock, right foot at 3 o'clock to the intended killing point. Mount the gun on to the killing point (rules permitting). Wind back along the line of flight to the point of first clear contact. Drop the butt from the face and shoulder, keeping the muzzles just under the anticipated line of flight. Turn the head slightly so that the eyes are directed to the area where you see the target as a blur or streak. Visualise the target breaking in your mind's eye. Call 'Pull!'—your eyes grab the target, the muzzles lock onto it. Without conscious effort they move in front . . . the trigger is pulled . . . the target is smoked . . . the gun barrels continue to move . . . .

Developing a shooting routine based on a sound basic technique and the principle of positive visualisation will immediately increase your percentage of kills. It will help you to identify mistakes by establishing a datum against which you can compare actual performance. Once a routine like this becomes truly habitual, you will progress to a new level of competence.

Forward allowance

As already observed, if you follow a systematic approach to shooting, one which puts special emphasis on preparation, you will not have to worry too much about lead on the great majority of targets as lead calculation will be regulated automatically. However, there will be some exceptions to the subconscious approach (though even these become fewer in number as one develops confidence in the subconscious system): very high driven birds, some long crossing targets, and some visually deceptive targets may require a more deliberate technique with some shooters. It will rarely amount to more than saying to oneself in the preparation phase 'This one needs a little [or a lot] extra' or 'I must make an effort to keep under this one'. *No precise measuring of the target will be required if you have the discipline to keep watching the bird*. Measuring rarely leads to consistent shooting—and is not advocated here—because the angle, speed and distance of sporting targets vary too much for the technique to be consistently applied. (The only time I tell someone to shoot 'a foot in front' or 'two feet in front' is when I am teaching a complete beginner who has no conception of forward allowance.)

Pairs

When shooting pairs, all the basics of Positive Shooting still apply—the core technique and the individual routine, and visualising a positive result before calling for the targets (although in this case seeing both targets being broken one after the other). So how are pairs different? They aren't really! Indeed, as A.J. Smith once noted 'There is no such thing as a pair', but always two separate targets to be assessed and shot—even when both birds seem to be moving in exactly the same direction.

When you are faced with a pair, the first thing to do (as always) is to watch very carefully. How different are the lines of the two birds? Does one drop off? Are they both travelling at the same speed? These are the important questions. As always, note the errors of others—can you see why they are going wrong? Can you see what you *should* be doing?

Which bird should be shot first? Let us imagine you are about to shoot a pair of simultaneously released crossers from a trap placed to your left. Normally you would shoot the rear bird first, but set up your stance according to where you want to take the *second* shot.

Why is the rear bird usually shot first? Because both targets can then be shot in a single flowing motion, so you do not have to move back and forth. Similarly, setting up the stance to favour the front bird aids smoothness, as you do not 'run out' of body movement when you come to shoot the second target.

Exceptions

Although the rear-bird-first technique works in 80–90 per cent of situations involving simultaneous pairs, there are occasions when you may have to shoot the front clay first—most notably, when the first target dominates your vision in spite of good visual discipline; or when leaving the first target would make the shot significantly harder (because it is dropping quickly or disappearing behind cover). When shooting 'the wrong way round', set up the stance to favour the more difficult bird.

Pairs on report

A pair on report from the same trap provides no special problems as long as you return to the point of visual pick-up, smoothly and quickly after the first shot.

Trailing pairs

A pair released from the same trap neither simultaneously nor on report, but one bird immediately after the other; they put some shooters off because they force a change in rhythm. As with pairs on report, the secret is to return to pick up the second target not only smoothly, but quickly. Usually the pick-up point will be substantially in front of the pick-up point for the first shot. Don't panic on these shots—you will probably have more time than you think.

Combinations on report

Birds on report from traps placed in different positions can present special problems, particularly when each target requires a significantly different foot position. Assuming that it is not practical to change your foot position between shots (though sometimes it is), the general rule is to set up the foot position to favour the killing point of the more difficult target. If this makes the swing really awkward on the other target, you may have to compromise.

Any other advice? When you have shot the first bird, return immediately to a preselected pick-up point/zone for the second shot. Those who succeed in competition on these mixed report stands usually do so because they put more thought into their preparation, especially into stance and visual pick-up.

Specific sporting targets

Just apply the technique precisely, and do not worry about the angles. Remember, though, killing and pick-up points are crucial. Never allow yourself to be sloppy as you set yourself up. Pick-up, and alignment of feet to killing, are as crucial to teal or rabbits as they are to a simple skeet-like crosser.

Gun-fit

The purpose of the Positive Shooting system is to maximise the individual's natural ability and to develop it from within a disciplined framework. To achieve this, a well fitted gun is vital—that is, a gun which naturally shoots just above the point where one is looking (classically, the pattern distribution should be about two-thirds high). To ascertain if your gun fits, you will need to shoot it at a pattern plate and at targets; when shooting at the plates do not be too deliberate, and make sure you have a clear mark to shoot at, otherwise you will get misleading results. (You may improvise pattern plates as long as you consider the safety requirements carefully—a solid backdrop or a 300-yard safety zone.)

One of the best ways to make sure your gun fits, also that you have no eyesight anomalies, is to go to a professional fitter. For those who begrudge the cost (and they are foolish), or those who do not have access to a professional (and they are rare), here is a simple but approximate test. Prove your gun empty. Close it, and apply the safety catch. Still bearing safety in mind, choose a point just above head-height to practise gun-mounting. Watch the point, glue your eyes to it, mount the gun. Bring the gun down. Now, watching the same point, mount the gun again, but this time as the gun comes up to your face and shoulder close your eyes. When the gun is fully mounted, open your eyes.

If you are looking up one side of the rib, or if you can see too little or too much of the rib, your gun-fit may be less than ideal.

Eye dominance

Knowledge of one's eye dominance is a crucial consideration for those who seek to improve their shooting, and is vitally important to gun-fit. Pick out a small but distinct spot on the wall or horizon, and without thinking about it, point at it with a finger-tip, keeping both eyes open. Now, shut your right eye (if you are right-handed)—has your finger moved out of alignment with your chosen spot? If so, you are probably *right* master-eyed; but if your finger appears to have stayed still, you are probably *left* master-eyed.

What does all this mean? If you are right-handed and right master-eyed, you have no problems; similarly if you are left-handed and left master-eyed. However, difficulties arise when one's 'handed-ness' and master eye are opposite. Thus a right-hander with a left master eye has a number of options: the easiest is to shoot off the right shoulder, dimming or closing the left eye as the gun is mounted (a procedure which allows the shooter to take advantage of binocular vision as visual contact is first established). Other alternatives include an eye patch or, if the shooter wears spectacles, a barrier-to-vision attached to the appropriate lens. Another option (which is easier than you might think) is to learn to shoot off the left shoulder. The expensive, and not necessarily the best solution is to acquire a cross-over stock gun.

Note, too, that there is more to the question of eye dominance than the simple discovery that someone is right or left eye dominant. A few people will have so-called central vision, where neither eye is truly dominant; others will have one eye only slightly more dominant than the other. These subtle differences in vision will have the effect of pulling the muzzles to one side of the target or the other if the shooter is in the habit of keeping both eyes open; moreover, they will normally require the assistance of an experienced instructor or gunfitter to diagnose.

Choke for sporting

Choke is the constriction at the muzzle end of the barrels. My best advice is not to worry about it too much—or indeed about any other technical aspect of your gun. Very few sporting birds are missed because of incorrect choking; ninety-nine out of a hundred times they are missed because the gun has been pointed in the wrong place. People often blame choking (like so many other things) as an excuse for poor technique.

What choking is best? 1/4 and 1/4 choke is ideal for sporting, 1/2 and 1/2 is another excellent combination; both will tackle any bird on a sporting shoot. My own preference is for 1/2 and 1/2 because it kills more decisively and gives the experienced shot confidence. I use my 32in, 1/2 and 1/2 gun for all the English disciplines—sporting, skeet and Down-the-Line.

Cartridges for sporting

A good cartridge is one which will shoot smoothly in your gun, be clean burning, and which will produce even patterns consistently. I find that modern light loads, 1oz (28g) and less, are more conducive to comfortable shooting than the older heavier loads, and produce kills every bit as good.

What about shot size? Shells loaded with no 8 shot are ideal for sporting; combined with 1/4 and 1/4 or 1/2 and 1/2 choke they will break anything on a sporting layout. If I cannot get 8s I use 71/2s for everything; by choice I only use 9s for skeet. Changing from 71/2s to 9s depending on the target, as some people do, only serves to divert one's attention—like the habit of changing chokes repeatedly. The Positive Shooting dictum is to keep everything simple, and keep the attention focussed on the bird.

Gun Choice

Again, it can be distracting to think too much about guns. I will risk only a few words here. My own preference for sporting shooting is for longer bar-relled guns because they point more precisely and, usually, control recoil better. Long, fairly heavy guns promote consistency in competition. Few of the best sporting shots use 28in or 271/2in guns—the majority now opt for 30in or 32in guns; though for the less experienced shooter there are some advantages to a shorter barrelled gun, which swings easily. However, for anyone who is serious about sporting, my advice is to get a longer gun: 30in is probably the best choice for most people, and I would only suggest the 32in if you are really sure it is what you want.

Conclusion

Gun-fit apart, technical considerations are relatively unimportant to good shooting; generally speaking, far too much energy is wasted on worrying about them. What really counts is practice based on a sound technique. To get the most out of your practice, keep a log or diary of your shooting; I also suggest that you shoot regularly with the same person, preferably someone who is a better shot then you. Using the triangle of universals—visual contact, balance and rhythm—and a little common sense, you will be able to help each other considerably. Remember:

Always select the point where you first see the target clearly so you will know precisely where to point your gun while awaiting the target.

Always select a killing point and set up your stance to address it.

Always visualise what you want to achieve—a kill—before calling.

Always maintain visual contact with the bird throughout the process of shooting—*lock your eyes to the bird no matter what.*

Michael Yardley is an author, sporting journalist, and qualified sporting coach with extensive experience at all levels. He has also developed a method, known as Positive Shooting, a simple-to-follow style which brings effective results.

Move, Mount, Shoot

Robin Scott

So you want to hit more targets? Of course you do, otherwise you wouldn't have bought this book and be reading it now! However, nothing in shooting ever comes easily, and although books and magazine articles of an instructional nature are often very good, the written word can only ever hope to fire your enthusiasm and your desire to improve. It can act as the catalyst, and it can help you identify the symptoms and suggest a course of treatment, but it can't hope to cure the problem. That is up to the individual, and how determined he or she is to improve. It's one thing *wishing* you could hit more targets but an entirely different matter actually *doing* something about it. You might find that only a slight change in technique is needed to bring about the desired transformation; but it could involve you in a great deal of time-consuming hard work.

First you must identify the things you find difficult; then draw up an action plan on how you are going to tackle them. And the best way of achieving long-lasting success is to set yourself attainable goals—if you don't you will find yourself rushing to every available club ground trying to 'shoot' your way past difficulties, some of which might not exist. Maybe you already know what action needs to be taken; maybe you are merely suffering setbacks on one or two particular targets. But if you really are perplexed as to why things are going wrong, then the best (some say the only) course of action is to consult a qualified coach.

Don't be afraid to seek the help of the more experienced, competent clay shooters, but do treat their advice with the utmost caution—a fair percentage of them don't really understand how *they* break targets, let alone know how to explain their technique in order to help anyone else! In other words, pick your instructor with care because if you don't, you could end up in an even worse muddle—and I speak from experience! One of the drawbacks to being editor of *Sporting Gun* magazine is that most shooting instructors, when they see me shoot, will insist on trying to cure the faults. In the early days this was all very flattering, but I soon realised that it wasn't always my shooting they were sorting out; more usually it was the teaching of an earlier coach and in fact my shooting suffered dearly.

Most people would go into a Sporting stand worried only by the targets—I used to get inside wondering which one of twenty methods I needed to put into action! Should I put all my weight on the front foot or spread it evenly between the two? Should I keep a straight left leg or 'break' it slightly? Did I need to take the muzzles right back to the trap or leave them somewhere out in front? Should I pull the trigger with the pad of my forefinger, or rest it in the crease of the first joint? And as for gun-fit . . .

My gun stock was lengthened, shortened, raised, lowered or cast depending on the dictates of the various people who professed to know all about this fascinating science. The only consistent line taken by all the instructors I had the good fortune to meet was that the gun muzzles should always come from behind the target. Only in this way, they said, could a shooter keep in close contact with a clay *and* get a clear idea of its line and speed. This, I soon discovered, was all very well, but nobody could answer the question every improver asks sooner or later: 'How much lead do I have to give a target to break it?'

The reply ran pretty much to form: 'You don't need to worry too much about this part of the equation because it's taken care of by speed of swing. You'll always get the right forward allowance if you squeeze the trigger as you accelerate through—and past—the target.' However, the trouble is, of course, no two shooters will swing the gun at the same speed, so where one says he gave a target 'a couple of feet lead' to break it, another will bring about its demise by shooting 'directly at it'.

'Don't worry about this' chime those helpful instructors 'with experience you get to know instinctively when you should pull the trigger.' This is true. Things get so much easier the more shooting you do.

It is also true that if you 'see lead' in terms of a gap between the gun and the target before the trigger is squeezed, then there's a very good chance you have slowed, or stopped, the gun at a very critical stage in the proceedings. If this happens you invariably miss behind—and we are told that you rarely miss in front. However, as most good instructors know only too well, it is actually very easy to miss in front.

Yet what happens when you miss a target which you *know* needs plenty of lead? Nine times out of ten you will tell yourself you missed it behind, and give it even more lead (probably by swinging the gun ever faster) on the next shot. Rarely will you stop and ponder the possibility that it was missed in front—and in this case, speed of swing can become a very destructive force indeed. Take a look at the shooters around you: there are those who throw their gun muzzles across the sky at break-neck speed, and others who point out targets with a stop–start motion that puts the shot charge anywhere and everywhere but on the bird. These are people on whom 'speed of swing' has backfired.

Undoubtedly those shooting techniques which rely on the gun being brought from behind, and up to the target, are amazingly effective and consistent when done properly. But there's more than one way to success—and the successful hit, in this instance, depends on forward allowance. Let us consider that, regardless of the technique you use, the object of the exercise is to place the shot charge in front of a moving target. Thus in real terms it should matter little how you contrive to get the gun into position in readiness for the shot; all that matters is that you can do it easily, consistently and with minimum physical effort.

This brings us nicely to the style of shooting known as Maintained Lead, developed and taught by former World FITASC Sporting Champion, John Bidwell at High Lodge Shooting School in Suffolk. John believes that the most consistent, and physically less taxing way of breaking targets is to keep the gun muzzles in front of the bird *at all times*; at no stage is the bird allowed to pass the line of the muzzles. More experienced shooters often find this concept difficult to accept—hardly surprising since it completely

John Bidwell in action. John has achieved great success with the maintained lead method

contradicts traditional thinking on the subject. And I must say, I too, was highly sceptical at first. 'Don't be silly,' I said 'everbody knows that you've got to come from behind a target to break it.'

So what changed my mind?

Over a six-month period I travelled with him to shoots far and wide, talked to him about the method he taught, and analysed the constituent parts of it; but, more telling perhaps, I also sat quietly as a spectator at innumerable lessons at High Lodge and watched pupils of all abilities being taught. To say the results he got were a revelation would be an understatement, and this was especially the case with beginners who had never fired a gun before. One particular day I wandered in mid-way through a lesson to see a middle-aged pupil smashing long-range midi-crossers from the high tower with consummate ease. He then went on to repeat the performance with rabbits and springing teal before his hour was up. After settling his bill and leaving the ground I asked John whether his pupil was a game shooter or regular Sporting competitor, just having a brush-up on targets he found awkward. 'Not at all,' came the reply 'he only took up shooting three weeks ago, and that's his second lesson.' There were many other, similar examples, too.

I suppose it was the ease with which people took to the technique, and also the sheer simplicity of the whole thing that caught my attention. As an added bonus it also sidestepped the confusing subject of 'speed of swing'. . . So how does the technique work? And how does the shooter ensure that his barrels stay ahead of the target?

Regardless of the speed, distance and angle of the target being tackled, a shooter need only follow three basic steps to keep in front and break the bird. First, he needs to decide where he wants to hit the target (this dictates his foot position); second, he must decide where he's going to see the target *clearly*; and third, he must address his unmounted gun muzzles to a point mid-way between the chosen pick-up and kill points.

If the gun is taken too close to the place where the target comes into view there's a danger that it will pass the barrels—or get too close to them—before the shooter starts to move the gun. If this happens he is once more relying on speed of swing to break the bird—or he could simply 'poke' at the target and miss it behind. On the other hand if the gun is held too far out, he is likely to mount the gun too early, leading (usually) to a miss in front; he might even end up waiting for the bird and trying to spot-shoot it as it closes the gap on his barrels.

Clearly, visual pick-up, muzzle position and killing point are critical.

The aim of the exercise is always to start moving the gun as soon as the target comes into clear view: *never* be tempted to base your approach to a shot on your first fleeting glimpse of the clay. Your response should always be geared to seeing the bird properly, otherwise inconsistencies in gun-mounting will set in. Keep both eyes firmly on the bird as you mount the gun, and shoot as soon as the stock finds your face and shoulder. It goes without saying that the gun must be kept moving after the shot has been taken.

The beauty of the technique is that it reduces wasteful gun movement because the shooter doesn't have to track his target from behind, come up to the bird, and then accelerate past it to get in front. With John's 'Move, Mount, Shoot' technique the necessary forward allowance is dialled in soon after the gun starts moving.

For those used to shooting one of the follow-through techniques, there is a natural reluctance to accept that the gun can come to the right place ahead of a target without the shooter having to speed up his swing a split second before the shot is triggered. Such reluctance is understandable because they have been taught that it is desirable to shoot with an accelerating gun muzzle and, more significantly, that only by coming from behind can 'the line of the target' be established.

John admits that he hasn't yet fathomed out how the human brain is able to judge speed instantly and transmit the answer to the hands guiding the gun. All he *can* say—quite rightly, too—is that hand-to-eye co-ordination will always put the gun in the right place *provided* the shooter doesn't inter-fere with the process.

But let us consider 'target line' for a moment. If you believe that speed and line can only be determined by tracking the bird in time-honoured fashion, then how do you explain a cricketer's ability to hit or catch a speed-ing ball, or a tennis player's knack of returning his opponent's high-velocity service? They do it, of course, by watching the ball and allowing natural co-ordination to bring their hand, or racket, to the right place every time. Exactly the same principles apply in shooting, only now the bat or racket is replaced by a gun. For those who are accustomed to another shooting technique, the difficulty lies in making themselves believe that they can achieve accurate assessment of forward allowance in this way. Often their well rehearsed mental and physical response to a target will interfere with the process by which lead is achieved using Bidwell's technique.

The basic problem here is that the 'sight pictures' which a shooter is used to, take on a new perspective. For instance, when a shooter is used to breaking a target with a fast-moving gun he expects to see it turn to dust with, say, a six-inch gap between the muzzles and the bird. Speed of swing prevents him from seeing the *actual* lead needed to break that bird, which (for argument's sake) wanted a full six feet. Yet that is what he would see if he were to break the same bird using Bidwell's technique. But because he isn't used to seeing lead in *real* terms, our shooter will be tempted to override the instructions arrived at through hand-to-eye co-ordination. Progress will only be made, however, if the shooter is prepared to trust in his God-given ability to co-ordinate.

By way of example I can relate a personal experience: three years ago in Cyprus I came up against a high, very fast, fifty-yard upside-down battue which most people were struggling to hit. Having decided where I wanted to kill the target I looked back up the mountain, put my gun in the recommended half-way position and called for the target. As it came into sight I started moving the gun. But it wasn't until the gun was in my shoulder that I realised, to my horror, that the barrels were about fifteen feet under the target and about the same distance in front. It was a weird, fleeting sight-picture that looked horribly wrong and I was tempted to stop the gun and let the bird catch up. Instead I fired—and caught the bird slap-bang in the centre of the pattern. I was so elated and unnerved by the whole thing that I then proceeded to miss the next three 'straightforward' birds! Complete beginners, however, take to the technique like ducks to water, for the simple reason that they do not know any different.

It isn't just 'sight pictures' which sometimes limit an experienced sportsman's acceptance of this technique: so, too, can his ingrained physical response when it comes to actually mounting the gun, because successful use of the 'Move, Mount, Shoot' style demands a speed of gun-mount which is positively slow compared to that often found in follow-through methods—in these, a shooter can't wait to get the stock to the shoulder so he can start tracking his bird. But such 'tracking' plays no part in the technique taught by John: he maintains that the peripheral view of a mounted gun rib interferes with the smooth movement of the muzzles as they are steered into place. Nothing, he says, should be allowed to hamper the view of the target once the gun starts to move. And to make absolutely sure it doesn't, he likes to see his pupils cultivate the habit of holding the muzzle just under the bird's flight-path and bringing the gun *up* to its line of flight. Certainly the gun should never be held too high because, when mounted, it could obscure the shooter's view of a target, causing him to slow the movement of the muzzles or forcing him to lift his head from the comb of the stock.

John's insistence that this technique of shooting has a valid place in the repertoire of all clay shooters has generated much heated discussion and argument over the years. And I doubt whether the differences of opinion will ever be settled. Unfortunately, much of the criticism levelled at this extremely successful shooter and shooting coach has totally missed the fundamental point that he is trying to make: that anybody who seriously wants to improve should be prepared to use techniques which suit the targets they will be expected to tackle in a normal day's shooting.

What John is really being criticised for is his proposal that some targets are much more easily broken by the method he prefers. Also, the fact that he (and a growing number of successful pupils) choose to use it on *most* of the birds they encounter has been taken as meaning, by inference, that other techniques are lacking in some way. This is certainly not the case, however, as John would be the very last person to try and change anyone's style of shooting if it was yielding good results.

Nonetheless, if a person is finding it a struggle to improve with one technique, then it must be in his interests to find out for himself whether a technique such as this is the key he has so long been looking for. To ignore the possibility that it might be the answer would be foolishness of the first degree.

Robin Scott (left) is the editor of Sporting Gun *magazine, and in conjunction with John Bidwell evolved and successfully promoted the Move, Mount, Shoot style of shooting which has brought success at all levels to many of its followers.*

5
Skeet Shooting

English skeet is an enjoyable discipline for many reasons. For the beginner it is good because it gives him the opportunity to break a few clays; it features a variety of targets from the straightforward to the awkward quartering shot; and it also stresses the importance of good gun-mount and approach work. For the serious competitor it offers a complete challenge because if he hopes to win a competition he must be sure that he can shoot a hundred straight. And while all targets can be broken easily enough with sufficient practice, it is a big enough hurdle putting one 25 straight together, let alone rattling out four on the trot.

It is also quite an addictive discipline. Quick initial progress is generally followed by a slower curve from 20 to 23, then slower still from 23 to 25 — though all along the way you know that next time out it will be different and you'll hit the lot!

English skeet is not identical to American (NSSA) skeet, but only varies inasmuch as there is a different sequence of singles and doubles on the seven stations; also, in American skeet they shoot the eighth station, at the midway point of the two trap-houses.

As the discipline was invented in the States where the top performers produce some prodigious scores, who better to give some advice than Ed Scherer? He competed in and won his first championship in 1947 with a borrowed gun and a score of 249 x 250, and since then the straights have never stopped coming—over a hundred in the last ten years alone, including five with a .410. He is a member of the Skeet Shooting Hall of Fame, and also has a Master's degree in education; thus his pedigree as a shooting instructor could hardly be better.

English Skeet Shooting

Ed Scherer

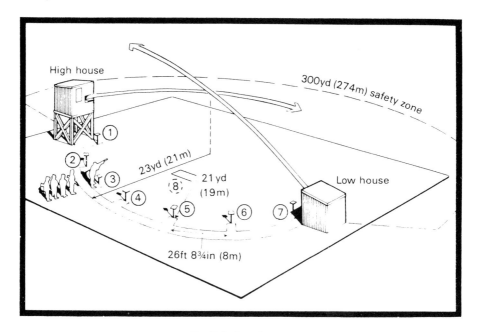

High house

300yd (274m) safety zone

① ② ③ ④ ⑤ ⑥ ⑦ ⑧

23yd (21m)

21 yd (19m)

Low house

26ft 8¾in (8m)

English skeet layout

In 1939 I had my initial exposure to skeet shooting, though the method used at that time to hit those elusive birds was not of concern. We just 'winged it'—if the target broke, so much the better, and if we missed it was still a mystery. Things have changed, and a million shots later this veteran skeeter has some news for all his British friends: there is a method, and it works.

We flew P-47 fighters in World War II, and when not flying, it was off to the skeet fields—and I certainly got in my share of skeet shooting. The method used then was swinging through the target; as you saw daylight, the trigger was pulled. I actually broke several 100 x 100s that way, shooting low gun and delayed targets. After World War II, however, Remington's great professional, Lee Braun, took me under his wing and stressed the maintained lead method. 'Ed,' he said, 'you want to ambush that target by staying ahead, never allowing the target to move ahead of the muzzle.'

The tubed over-under, used to shoot the smaller gauges, finally set the record straight. The tubes are heavy and didn't lend themselves to the swing-through method, and since every top shooter in the 1980s shot the fabulous tubes, the constant lead method surged to the fore-front.

Today, the great majority of our All-Americans use the maintained lead method, and everyone is equipped with tube sets. A tube set is a 12-gauge over-under with a full length set of smaller gauge tubes inserted inside the 12-gauge barrels. Jess Briley's tubes are the best: Briley, from Houston, Texas, decided if tubes were to be used, there had to be a better way to manufacture them. The original Purbough tubes had a separate set of extractors for each gauge and it was a nightmare to change tubes, especially with the popular Perazzi over-unders. Briley decided to build the extractor right into the tubes, so that all one had to do was line up the tube's extractor with the over-under's extractors and tap them in place.

My British friends shoot only the 12-gauge at skeet so the tubed over-under may not interest them—but it should, as the tubes pioneered and perfected the maintained lead method. Since tubed over-unders shoot best when the lead is maintained, the Americans also shoot the maintained method when switching back to the 12-gauge autoloaders in the 12-guage event—and that's where my British friends come in.

There is that all-important double at station 4 to be hit in each round of English skeet, and the maintained method gives instant results. Watch the All-Americans in their doubles shoot-offs at stations 3, 4 and 5 and you will see they all use the maintained method. They shoot the first target, slam on the brakes and hit the second before an eye can be blinked—the best shots maintain the lead on the second shot, and that's the key to victory.

Now let's see how a double at four is shot with a swing-through shot. The problem with this one is the delay in getting off the second shot. By the time the swing-through shot is completed on the first shot at four doubles, the second target is making a speedy exit. On a windy day, the second target may be hitting the ground about the time your second swing-through shot is fired. As for constant leading the second shot, it just can't be done that way.

The great Wayne Mayes said, a decade ago, and it's just as true today: 'How can we memorise the leads on a skeet target with the swing-through method, when the lead is always changing?' Skeet today is a matter of memorising the leads on each skeet station, and it's a lot easier to memorise a lead if it's not changing, such as in the maintained lead method. Skeet shooting is pulling the trigger when the maintained leads appear correct to the shooter; if he has done his homework and memorised the leads, those hundred straights are just around the corner. Unfortunately, a new skeeter has to burn lots of ammunition to learn the leads properly, but that's what it takes to excel.

If the best American skeeters use maintained lead in their doubles shoot-offs, there is bound to be a spill-over for regular skeet. The top shots end up shooting all the skeet stations with the maintained lead method, and the key to learning it is this: move the 'hold' point out. This is where the muzzle is placed in calling for the target. Set a stack of targets 19 feet out from the face of the skeet house, under the flight of target: this is your 'hold' point from now to eternity, and don't compromise!

On the high house targets, move the eyes back from the muzzle 'hold' point until you are gazing at a space halfway between the muzzle and the opening where the target emerges. On the low house the background is often cluttered with trees, so I suggest you look directly into the opening when calling for targets. On low 4,5 and 6 this little tip will really pay off. The muzzle should always be pointed a foot below the height of the emerging target.

Now that we've told you where to point the muzzle and where to look, what's next? Start the muzzle as the bird emerges, and do not compromise. If needs be, dry-fire a dozen shots, or better yet, put the skeet gun away and use an extended left arm (for right-handed shooters) to practise your 'starts'. The key is, never to allow a target to move ahead of the gun barrel. It can be done, as the top USA shooters do it every day (left-handers use their right hand to point).

Keep the head well down and the gun moving for those left-to-right crossers

Once the 'start' phase is completed, it's a matter of practice until the sight picture for each shot is memorised. However, as each target is thrown at the same speed, height and angle, why can't the lead be memorised? You are not shooting sporting clays where each target presentation is different. Here's an idea: the leads at low 3, high 4, low 4, and high 5 skeet stations are three feet. Cut a board three feet long and lay it on the ground on edge so that the three-foot lead can be visualised in the area where the target is broken. This will help on the tough wide-angle shots. All the other leads are less, so cut back. High 2 and low 6 take but a foot lead, so remember to cut back on these elusive targets. Enlist the help of a friend who can call your misses; this will help to save ammunition.

Finally, let me say this: the rules allow a premounted gun when calling for the target, so take advantage of this rule. Todd Bender, the number one skeet shooter in the world, broke 1400 straight tournament skeet targets last year without a miss for a 100 per cent average in the 12-gauge tournaments he entered. The key to his success is that he shoots with both eyes open; he shoots only a tubed over-under (he shoots a tubed 20-gauge in the 12-gauge events); he maintains the lead on each skeet target; and finally, he pre-mounts the gun before the target appears. What else can I say?

Station 1

For those of you who prefer the low gun position, there is no objection. I learned the hard way some twenty-five years ago when I was defeated in a shoot-off for a major championship. The man beating me kept his gun to his shoulder as he called for the target; I dropped the stock. From then on, it was gun to the shoulder when calling 'Pull' and, yes, it's actually easier. My misses in sporting are usually due to mismounting my gun, so why not eliminate the gun-mount in skeet and rid yourself of a potential miss; the rules in English and NSSA skeet do allow a gun to be mounted when calling for the target.

The muzzle should be up at a 30° angle with the ground, and eyes should be looking up and away from the muzzle on High One. I ask my students to actually gaze at the blue sky or even a cloud. A friend gave me a valuable sporting shooting tip, too, when he told me 'Always come up on a target, not down to it,' as he watched me shoot. From that day on I changed.

In the past, the muzzle was considerably higher as I'd come down through the target but over the years High One has always caused me grief. I have stuck with the new method and it works.

If you are accustomed to holding a high gun, and you switch to a lower hold point, it will be a bit scary, but stay with it. The best way to describe hitting High One is to let the bird come to you. Very little muzzle movement is needed, and be quite certain that the cheek is frozen on the comb as the shot is fired.

High One is a very unforgiving target, as are most straight-aways, so keep your head down. On a day when a tail wind is pushing the target down, the lower hold point will be a blessing. The key is never to lose sight of the target—if it suddenly jumps up because of the wind, just move the muzzle up and blast it.

There should be just a tiny bit of light under the target as you fire—I used to tell my students to hold the muzzle six inches below the target in firing, but I find that's too much.

Here's a tip that has paid dividends for me: as I pull the trigger, I actually freeze my cheek to the stock and count 'one thousand one' to myself after the shot, and only then take my head off the comb. We shoot lots of .410s in the USA with its unforgiving small pattern, and a frozen cheek on the stock pays high dividends.

You may find it difficult to keep your cheek on the stock after the shot because of excessive recoil; the new 25g load could be the answer if we can convince the manufacturer of cartridges to cut that muzzle velocity to 1200 feet per second. 1400 feet per second is great for trap shooting and long-range sporting targets, but at 21 yards on a skeet field the slower velocities are better. The 25g load is approximately 7/8oz of shot, and is a similar load to the standard 20-gauge load used in NSSA skeet.

The 25g load in 12-gauge, however, is more efficient ballistically than the 20-gauge load. The bigger the hole, the more efficient the load. Last year the NSSA shooters averaged 99.73% on their 20-gauge targets (a composite average of the top ten shooters), while the top ten 12-gauge skeeters averaged 99.74%. And all those 20-gauge averages among the top ten were compiled with a tubed 20-gauge fitted inside a 12-gauge barrel.

There's a spot five yards before the crossing point at Station 8 (midway between high and low) that seems to be the best place to break High One. Have a friend watch as you shoot, and ask him (or her) to stand to the right of Station 2 to tell you where you broke the target: be sure to break the single in the same place as the first shot in the double. We all tend to rush the first shot in doubles.

Low One takes a small six-inch lead and is best broken half-way between the crossing point and high house. In calling, I place the muzzle half-way between the low-house opening and Station 8. On all low houses, it is best to look into the opening; under lights, Low One could be tricky as only the dark underside is visible.

Other shots are not affected as much as High One if the target height is incorrect. Check target height before starting and ask the club to 'hoop' the target before shooting to assure proper height. Do this as a starter. On a separate skeet field, have a friend vary the height of the target to simulate windy conditions. This is a great exercise and you'll be thankful for the lower hold point for the muzzle. (The term 'hold point' means where the muzzle is held when calling for the target.)

Check your foot position; feet should never be more than a foot apart, and the front knee should be slightly bent with no more than 60 per cent of your weight on the front foot; the back knee should be kept firm. Have the navel facing the low-house opening and your left foot pointing at the 'sweet' spot (where the target is broken). Left-handers should have their navel facing away from the skeet field with the right foot and toes pointing toward the 'sweet' spot.

Do you have a white knuckle grip? Loosen up. As for the double, break the first shot where the single was broken, but shoot the second shot of the double a bit later than the single. The bottom line in skeet is to pull the trigger when you are seeing the correct sight picture. However, to memorise the correct sight picture on each station does take a bit of practice.

Station 2

The novice experiences more problems on High Two than any other skeet station; and those of you just switching to the fabulous tube sets may find your problems aggravated. However, High Two can be hit, and with consistency, but it takes an extra effort.

The hold point (where the muzzle is pointed when calling for the target) is critical. If the muzzle is back too far, towards the opening, the bird will run off and leave you, thus requiring a swing-through shot. Move the hold point out too far and swing will be lost, leading to a dead or stopped muzzle as the trigger is pulled.

For your practice rounds, place a stack of twelve targets on the ground at the hold point to ensure the same exact starting-point each time—whatever your age or reactions, the hold point does not change. The High Two skeet target, on a properly built skeet field, will always travel sixty yards. It must also pass directly over the a marker placed where the two targets from the low- and high-houses cross. So if the target is required to cross over the marker each time and the distance it travels in still air is sixty yards each time, why attempt to change the muzzle hold point or the one foot lead required?

If your skeet field does not have a sixty-yard marker, then you should insist that one is put there. The same applies to a marking stake at the target crossing point. Only with these two in place can you attempt to break a consistent score on a skeet field.

The hold point is located nineteen feet out from the face of both the low and high skeet-houses, directly under the target path. Make certain that when measuring where to place the hold-point marker on both the high- and low-houses the tape measure is placed directly under the target opening; it should touch the face of the skeet-house at ground level.

Footwork is the next concern. Have your navel face the low-house opening for both the high- and low-houses and for the double. Everyone fudges on my foot position, but *don't*: it is not to be compromised, and neither is the hold point. To keep you from cheating, follow this procedure: imagine that a line crosses the tips of your toes, and another goes off at a 90° right angle from it. This second line, which is right below your navel, should run exactly into the low skeet-house target opening.

The muzzle should be placed over the stack of targets, which is the hold point for the high-house target. The muzzle should be just high enough so the departing high-house target (I call it the zipper as it appears so fast) travels a foot above it. It's always safer to come up on a target than to come down through it; better you start below High Two.

Eyes next: where to look to pick up this one? Certainly not over the muzzle, or this departing 'zipper' will get a head start. With the head firmly in place on a pre-mounted gun, roll the eyes to the left to a spot halfway between the muzzle and the target opening. Loosen the grip on the forearm to ensure a smooth start. When the bird appears, start the muzzle immediately and set up a one foot lead. Just a few feet before the crossing point at station 8 and after you have seen that correct one foot lead, pull the trigger, keeping the head frozen on the comb *after* the shot is fired.

As you see the target break, you are now ready to set up the one foot lead required for the second shot of the double, which, is taken a bit later than Low Two single. If executed properly, both shots use the constant or maintained lead method. The second shot of the double takes less lead than Low Two single because it's slowed up more.

Be prepared on High Two to use the swing-through method should it run off and leave you, but it now takes less apparent lead. The worst problem on swinging through High Two on a swing-through shot is that the, muzzle is out of control—it will be swinging too fast and 95 per cent of your misses will be overleading the target.

Before actually attempting a shot at High Two, put your gun down and simulate a shot using your left arm only. Point the index finger of an extended left arm over the hold point. Look halfway back toward the opening, and simulate shooting a dozen targets this way; as you proceed with the exercise you will find it gets easier to start the arm moving smoothly as the bird appears, and soon you will be maintaining the required lead.

Next, put the snap caps in your skeet gun and dry-fire another dozen shots with a pre-mounted gun and cheek firmly in place on the comb as you call for target. I'll wager a pound that if the above dry-firing is done properly, the first time a live shell is put in your skeet gun, a hit will result.

On Low Two single, place the muzzle in an area halfway between the low-house opening and the crossing point. As the bird comes in view, start the muzzle moving immediately to ensure it is always in front of the target. Set up an 18in lead, and pull the trigger as the target is halfway between the crossing point at 8 and the high-house opening. Freeze your head on the comb one second after the shot is fired. Remember, always keep your eye on the target, and never look back to the muzzle.

And once again to emphasise that you *can* pre-mount a shotgun before calling for target, Todd Bender does and in 1991 he shot at 5,750 targets in all four gauges and only missed 16, to set a new four-gun world record average of 99.714 per cent. Not only does he pre-mount his gun and keeps this face firmly in place on the stock as he calls 'pull', he also shoots a tubed over-under and maintains the lead on *every* shot.

Station 3

High Three seems fast when first viewed, but if the correct instructions are carefully followed it can be hit with consistency. Leave your skeet gun in the rack and extend your left arm, as you did on skeet station 2. For the left-handed skeeter, extend your right arm: with the index finger pointed over the hold point (a stack of targets placed nineteen feet out from the face of the skeet-house but directly under the flight of target), gaze at a spot halfway between the hold point and the target opening. When 'Pull' is called make a concerted effort to start your arm moving immediately as the target appears. Do *not* start on the call: start only when the bird appears.

Repeat this procedure at least a dozen times; as you continue this exercise the swing will get smoother, and starting the swinging arm as the bird appears will get better. High Two, High Three and Low Six appear faster than any target, but despair not—they can be hit with plenty of practice.

Let's put some snap caps in our over-under (the Remington 1100, 11-87 and Beretta autoloaders do not require snap caps) and dry-fire this shot another twelve times before actually attempting a shot. The great advantage of this dry-firing exercise is that the novice can spot why he missed, which is a great help. By now you must be wondering just how much lead High Three requires: try two feet.

The sight picture on Station 3 high house – maintain a two-foot lead and pull the trigger as the target crosses the halfway stage between the two houses

We're ready for that first shot. The navel points towards the low-house opening and this automatically puts your feet in the proper position. Probably you've never faced around to the right that far, but if it feels strange, fine—that means a new method is being employed, and it also means a better hit will be made on that high three zipper.

Eyes halfway back from the muzzle and where the bird emerges; loosen the forward hand holding the fore-arm, ensuring a smooth start. As the zipper appears, start immediately and set up the required two feet lead. When things go right, High Three should be broken with a maintained two-feet lead before the crossing point out there at station 8. I take the high bird three quarters the distance from the target opening and the crossing point.

If trouble develops on High Three, the temptation is to change the hold point. *Don't*. Stick it out with that 19ft hold point but be more alert so the muzzle can be started as the bird appears. Even if the target is broken with the maintained lead, there is a time or two when it runs off and leaves me, in spite of my best intentions to maintain the lead. A swing-through shot is the only salvation, so in this instance use it.

A word of caution: it will take less lead as muzzle speed is faster than that of the target, but this just isn't the way to hit any skeet target consistently. Once the maintained method is learned, with more practice than you ever imagined, it will prove to be the best—ask any of the great American skeeters how they hit their 100s, from Wayne Mayes and Todd Bender to all the up and coming talent.

The bottom line is this: shoot enough practice, and you'll memorise the two-foot lead required on high three; but if it's a swing-through shot the lead will never be learned because it's always changing.

For some reason there is more head-lifting when High Three is shot than any other. Have a friend stand just to your right and observe the cheek as shot is fired. If this is a problem, perhaps a softer recoiling shell will help, as excessive recoil is one of the biggest causes of a lifted cheek as shot is fired.

Todd Bender shoots only a tubed 20-gauge in the 12-gauge events; so do I, so does Robert Paxton, Gabby Hulgan, Luke Deshotel and many other All-Americans. We learned a long time ago that reducing recoil and adding weight (tubes) to the skeet gun pays dividends.

Let's tackle Low Three. Visualise a three-foot lead, as that's what it will take to hit this wide crosser. Do not tarry, or a head wind will cause a disaster. It should be taken near that crossing point at eight. Carry that target too far across the skeet field, and a slowed muzzle will give problems—five feet past the crossing point is far enough. Be aggressive and attack it.

The muzzle on Low Three must be exactly over the hold point placed nineteen feet out from the face of the house. It's time now—the eyes are looking very near that opening, but as we proceed around the skeet field on low 4, 5 and 6, be sure they look right into the opening as you call 'Pull!'. And if you've never tried looking into the opening, make sure you do soon because it will pay off, rest assured.

Station 4

Station 4 is the most important skeet station on the skeet field; both a double and two singles are fired here.

The singles

A stack of targets placed nineteen feet out from both the high and low houses, under the target flight, will serve as a reference or hold point where the muzzle is pointed when calling for target.

Arriving on station 4, the navel must be pointing at the low-house opening; this will properly position the feet so that when the trigger is pulled, the swing will continue. The left-handed skeeter uses the high-house opening as the reference point. Since both targets are broken near station 8, the navel remains pointed at the low-house opening on both the high- and low-house shots. You've never used your hips that much before, have you?

The front knee is slightly bent, with the back knee firm. As the High Four target emerges, the forward knee starts a turn to the right with the body and swinging shotgun following.

Using the body instead of just the arms produces a smooth swing, so essential on the skeet field. I'd place sixty per cent of my weight forward, with feet a shoulder-width apart, no more.

We're trying to prevent the inevitable sway on this high-house target that causes so many problems. The bent, turning knee should cause only a twisting motion, and enlist a friend to ensure the head does not move sideways. Invariably on that sway the shoulder drops and the cheek comes off the comb as the shot is fired. A video camera zeroed in on the shoulder area as shot is fired replaces a thousand words, and will certainly detect the sway. What fun to observe yourself on a TV screen for the first time. You might even decide to shed a few pounds!

With a pre-mounted gun held over the hold point make certain that the muzzle height is below the target path as the call is made. At least a pre-mounted gun eliminates one variable—a mismounted shotgun. How many sporting targets have been missed with a mismount?

Eyes should be looking between the hold point and the high house. As the bird emerges, *start* the gun muzzle moving immediately so as to remain in front of the targets throughout the shot.

The high-house target travels the same speed each time plus the same angle and height, so a skeeter will soon memorise the three-foot lead required to hit this target. Why swing through the bird when it's a lot easier to ambush it? Granted, we all seem to have used the swing-through method when first learning skeet shooting, but as skill improves the muzzle is gradually moved out so as better to execute the maintained lead. It takes many shots to memorise the sight picture on each target, but in the end it will all be worthwhile. That elusive 100 x 100, once it's broken, will be worth all the effort expended.

If high four can be broken just prior to station 8, so much the better. In the double it needs to be broken there, so why not for the single?

The bottom line in skeet is to pull the trigger when seeing the correct lead. If the muzzle is moving at exactly the same speed as the target, and the head remains glued to the comb as shot is fired, you will hit each and every target. There are no mysteries in breaking the 100s, just hard work, constant practice and a good memory.

Here's a tip to help you memorise the leads at station 4, but you will need a stake at the target crossing point. Since a three-foot lead is required, take two stacks (again they must be placed under the flight of the target, the same as the stack used for the hold point). With the two stacks in place and while standing on station 4, point the muzzle at the base of the crossing stake and look to the left: notice the space between the crossing stake and the stack of targets three feet to the left—project that same space into the sky as the shot is fired, and the target will be hit.

Low Four is a challenging shot, and a rank beginner should try a blend shot. Move the muzzle slightly closer to the trap opening. As the trigger is pulled, use a slight swing-through shot, increasing the lead as shot is fired. As your skills increase, gradually move out the hold point until the muzzle is directly over the 19ft marker. The highly skilled use the maintained three-foot lead and shoot the target before station 8. Later we'll show how important shooting it faster helps in the double.

Use the same foot position, with the navel still facing the opening as used on the high house. The background always seems cluttered unless shooting over water, so I advise looking directly in the target opening so as better to observe this challenging target. Remember to start the muzzle moving immediately the target emerges, with a loose grip on the fore-arm to ensure a smooth start.

Point the muzzle at the centre stack of targets placed at eight, and study the distance between the centre target and the one three feet to the right; simulate this space in the sky when firing, and the target will be broken *provided that* a smooth swing is maintained and your cheek is frozen on the comb one second after the shot is fired. If your head comes off the stock as the shot is fired, it could be from excessive recoil.

Low-house shots for the right-handed shooter seem to take less physical effort because the muzzle is pulled with the left hand. The high-house shot previously required is pulled with the left hand, and takes more effort.

The Americans load two shells on singles and it seems to speed up the game. Originally, for safety reasons, one shell only was allowed, but I've seen no serious problems this past decade. Besides, I'd rather put my effort into hitting targets instead of loading guns.

The double

The wind should always decide which target is shot first with the double at four. Usually the high-house target is sent crashing into the ground, pushed by a north wind, and then the high house should be taken first in the double. In the case of the 1991 British Open there was a south wind, and consequently at station 4 competitors should have chosen the first shot as their low house. The high house, slowed considerably because of the stiff breeze it faced, was an easier shot than usual.

In this situation I would advise cutting back the lead on the second shot, by about half. Here's why. Taking the high house first on a calm day will give you a slowed target on the second shot as it's taken a bit later. The low-house target has been climbing, and that will slow any target.

More importantly, the angle of the target is less, presenting a small quartering shot instead of a full deflection shot as in the single. My guess is that the low-house target is now presenting the skeeter with a 45° angle shot instead of a 90° shot; that in itself requires less lead, besides the fact that it is a slower target, due to it being later.

There is another factor to consider: half of you will be taking it so late that a swing-through shot will be used, and that will also involve less lead. So when you miss, you've probably overled. I shot the low house first in the 1991 British Open, and I can still see the High Four I overled on the last round because the wind had slowed it.

Here's a tip I use when teaching doubles: shoot the second target only. Here's the procedure: suppose you want to learn the sight picture for the low house, which you've elected as the second shot. Point the gun muzzle directly over station 8 because that's where the muzzle will be after the high house has been taken.

Look over the barrel and call for the low-house target. It will be past station 8 when it's shot and while shooting it, note the smaller lead required to score a hit. I'd suggest about a dozen shots like this to impress on your mind the smaller lead required.

If you've elected to take the high house as the second shot, the same procedure can be used to learn about the smaller lead required for high four.

See you in the shoot-off!

Station 5

The grass is always greener around station 5 from the tears shed here. It's a tough one and it needs an extra effort on your part, so here are some valuable tips.

Footwork is critical for the high house, so make certain your navel is looking right into the opening of the low-house target; left-handed shooters need to have the navel pointed towards the high-house opening. Turn your hips into this high-house target so that when the trigger is pulled, the hips are unwinding, assuring you of a continued, *level* swing. Too often skeet shooters face where the target appears, *not* where it's shot, so they lose the swing and the body compensates by dropping the right shoulder just as shot is fired. This usually results in a missed target underneath. If I were to video you just as the high-house shot is fired, we would soon see if the head turned or swayed when the shot was fired, if the shoulders were level or if they dipped. If they did, you're in trouble! I want to see a level swing, but more importantly, no sideward movement of the head—the head must turn when following the skeet target, but no side sway, please.

The 'sweet spot' is a term borrowed from a friend, John Bidwell, and describes where the target is best broken. After shooting a million shots on a skeet field in 54 years, this writer has determined that the sweet spot for the high house is past the crossing spot out there at station 8. Most of our better shots break it at least three to five yards past the crossing point, and a three-foot lead does the trick.

Set a stack of targets nineteen feet out from the high house, directly under the flight of the target. This is where the muzzle should point when calling for the target. Look halfway back towards the target opening from your muzzle. As the bird emerges, start the muzzle swinging immediately and set up a three-foot lead. You must be careful not to start on the call: discipline yourself to start *when the bird emerges*, not on the call.

Most British shooters use the swing-through shot on this high-house target, and it does work fairly well; but here's the problem: on the swing-through shot, the lead is constantly changing, so how are you going to learn the correct lead? If the hold point is moved out to the nineteen-foot mark, and if the muzzle moves immediately the target emerges, it will eliminate the swing-through shot. The top notchers in the USA maintain a three-foot lead on the shot every time, and the best way to learn what this three-foot lead looks like is to persuade a friend who can spot your misses to stand behind and watch as the shot is fired. As he calls the miss, make your lead adjustment. Once the target is hit, remember that sight picture and shoot another dozen shots until the sight picture is etched indelibly in your mind.

Low Five is the typical quartering shot and is easily overled, especially when taken out further. Again, erect a stack of targets nineteen feet out from the low-house opening; look directly into the mouth of the trap opening when calling. As the bird emerges, start the muzzle immediately and when a two-foot lead is placed on this target, fire. No need to rush this shot.

Here's a valuable tip on Low Five: as I pull the trigger, I pull away slightly from the target, assuring me of a swinging muzzle as I fire. For some reason most of my skeeter friends slow the muzzle as the shot is fired; a slight pull-away shot will prevent this. I would almost consider this a blend shot, where the constant lead method is combined with a pull-away shot. Certainly it works, so give it a try.

More advice: have a friend stand to your right, to make sure that your cheek remains on the comb as the shot is fired—Low Five is an easy shot for head-lifting.

The left-handed shooter must peer right into the low-house opening as the target is called for, and both eyes must be open or this rascal will run off and leave him.

See you in the shoot-off.

Station 6

High Six is my training target, and is an excellent choice for a first target shot in the skeet shooting schools; it is the perfect target for introducing students to the maintained-lead method of hitting a skeet target. All new students can start here versus low seven. High Six teaches lead, swing and alignment, which are the basics of all shotgunning; Low Seven, being a straight-away shot, is difficult and certainly leaves a lot to be desired as a training shot because swing and lead are not taught here.

Erect the hold-point stack of a dozen targets nineteen feet out from the face of the skeet-houses (measure from directly under the opening) and make certain the stack is directly under the flight of the target. With muzzle over the stack, gaze halfway between muzzle and target opening; in height, the muzzle should be level with the bottom of the opening. As the target emerges, you should be setting up a two-foot lead—the lead will be set up if the muzzle starts moving immediately the bird appears. I'm always reminding my students to start their swing as the target emerges, *not* when it has passed the gun barrel.

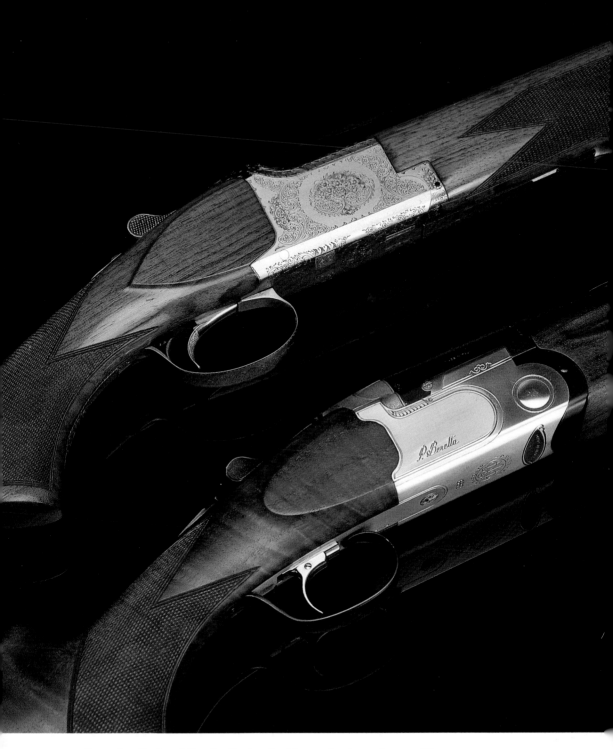

Browning (top) and Beretta: the two best known makers of competition guns

This photograph shows the shot string and wad immediately after being fired at a trap target

Barry Simpson, one of Britain's best known and most respected shots, is pictured 'getting into' a target

The only way a skeeter will ever learn the correct, maintained two-foot lead is to practise at least a dozen hits in a row so that the sight picture is memorised. After all, that is what skeet shooting is all about, memorising the leads, because unlike sporting clays, skeet targets fly the same path each time at the same angle, speed and height. The top shots have done their homework and have a two-foot sight picture in mind, memorised by practising. When that sight looks correct, the target is shot halfway between the station 8 crossing point and the low house.

Beginners always seem to slow their muzzle as the maintained-lead type of shot is consummated. Tell yourself to keep pushing through this shot, as a slightly slowed swing will result in a behind-the-target shot. Enlist the entire body in this shot, as you just did on high five. Face the low-house opening, then turn your hips back towards the area where the bird appears. Your hips will unwind as the shot is fired, and this will guarantee a continued swing as the target is broken at the half-point between the crossing point at station 8 and the low house.

Freeze you head on the comb as the shot is fired, and have a friend stand slightly to your right to observe whether your cheek *was* firmly pressed to

Station 6 low house is easily missed – sustain the concentration

the comb. If the head is lifted, there could be excessive recoil problem which must be addressed before any progress can be made.

Using the same foot position as that used on the high house, point the muzzle over the low-house hold point, which must be erected nineteen feet from the face of the low-house opening, under the flight of the target. A dry-fire exercise is needed on this shot, perhaps a dozen dry-fires. Peer directly into the low-house opening as the bird emerges, and start the swing immediately. After a dozen dry runs on this toughy, insert a shell in your favourite skeet gun and when you see a one-foot mainted lead, fire. Most reasons for missing are overleading and shooting under the target—remember to bring the muzzle up to the target just as the trigger is pulled. If misses still occur, you are almost certainly still overleading.

The double

The challenging double at six is a real test of mental discipline. Most hurry the first shot, stop their muzzle and rush to shoot the second shot: self-discipline tells us to see the low-house break before any attempt is made on the second shot. This important tip will eventually allow for the 100 x 100 we are all seeking.

The second shot is made leading with a bent front knee, turning to the right; the body follows the knee and swing is improved. A friend standing behind should observe your head: if there is a lot of sideways movement, there will be trouble! Many is the time in my shooting school that I have actually pushed my fists into the ribs of the skeeter to prevent the sideways movement. It works!

The second shot of six double requires less lead than the single as it is taken a bit later; the target has slowed, therefore lead is cut from two feet to one and a half. The head must remain frozen on the gun stock throughout the double.

Station 7

A one-foot lead will suffice on the high seven target, which is often thought to be the easiest of them all—but beware! Take this shot for granted and it will be missed. Just as the trigger is pulled on a one-foot lead, make certain the muzzle is high enough; novices tend to shoot under this rising target.

Are you looking at the gun muzzle as the trigger is pulled? If you are, it could mean a miss because the rule in shotgunning is to watch only the target; let the human brain do the rest. Try practising this exercise: look into a mirror—with your thumb upright, point it at your nose. The thumb simulates the shotgun barrel, while the nose is the target. Keep looking at your nose (target) in the mirror while moving the thumb (gun barrel) back and forth; note how you can see the thumb move while still looking at the target. This is exactly how a shotgun should be pointed: never look at the thumb, just the nose. If you switch your eyes to the thumb, the nose

Top shooter Duane Morley makes no mistake on the final bird for 25 straight.
It may look simple enough on the last station but there is no such thing as an easy bird

disappears; this invites a miss as we have now taken our eyes off the target.

Shoot this high-house target with a one-foot lead halfway between the midway point and the low house.

Low Seven can be tricky on a windy day. I suggest you allow the target to approach within five yards of midway point before the trigger is pulled; this allows the shot pattern to spread. Freeze your head on the comb of the gun stock. If the target dips or rises because of the wind, go down or up with the muzzle, assuring a hit. It's a dangerous policy to shoot the target before it dips or rises, as the pattern will not have enough time to open.

On the double, the low house is shot where the single is shot, whereas the second shot of the double is shot closer in than the single high shot. Extra caution is needed on the high-house target as pattern spread is at a minimum. Freeze your head on the comb.

The high house is your option for the 25 straight. Loosen your grip on the fore-arm to assure a smooth swing, and if you're coming in with a 100 x 100, be prepared for your team-mates to shoot your hat as it's thrown into the air. Rest assured, you'll do well in the shoot-off.

Olympic Skeet Shooting

Jim Sheffield

Olympic skeet, or ISU skeet as it was called in this country until very recently, is the type of skeet shooting which is notably carried out in Olympic Games competitions. It is shot in accordance with rules developed by the International Shooting Union (ISU), a body which administers international competitive shooting worldwide.

The reader is to be forgiven if, as his interest in shooting develops, he becomes somewhat confused by the fact that he will inevitably encounter other forms of skeet shooting, particularly in this country. These other varieties are 'English skeet', the domestic discipline of the sport shot extensively at club and national level throughout Great Britain; and 'NSSA skeet', a close cousin with its origins in North America where skeet shooting was invented in the 1920s. English skeet is administered by the Clay Pigeon Shooting Association (CPSA), whose headquarters are at Buckhurst Hill in Essex. In this country, Olympic skeet is administered by the CPSA's British International Board (BIB). NSSA skeet's administration is based in San Antonio, Texas.

Olympic skeet and the other forms of skeet mentioned share certain similarities in that the shooting ranges are identical and the targets are thrown in the same directions. However, the order of shooting the targets is a little different, and changes again after 1 January 1993! (We will go into this in more detail later). Besides that, the Olympic skeet targets fly significantly faster, travelling some 67 metres; targets are released with a random variable delay of up to three seconds, rather than instantaneously after a competitor calls for a target; and competitors are denied the freedom to call for targets with a mounted gun, and instead must adopt a position where a part of the gun butt is in contact with the hip-bone when calling for a target. This position must be maintained until the target emerges from the trap-house. These factors contrive to make Olympic skeet harder than the other varieties, a fact not lost on those charged with the responsibility of administering competitions for the world's best skeet shooters.

Olympic Skeet Equipment

So what do you need to be able to start shooting Olympic skeet? Let us first consider the equipment.

The skeet gun

The rules allow the use of any shotgun not bigger than 12-bore, and capable of firing two shots in fairly rapid succession. This provides for a choice between a double-barrelled gun and one which is semi-automatic. While there is nothing to prevent a side-by-side double-barrelled gun being used, these are very uncommon these days in skeet-shooting circles, the preference amongst the majority of skeet exponents being an over-and-under. Some shooters favour semi-automatic guns, and results over the years have shown these to be just as capable of producing winning scores as the more popular over-and-unders.

If you have not already got a gun, how might you go about looking at the advantages and disadvantages of each type?

Semi-automatic shotguns, particularly those which operate on a gas-bleed principle, tend to produce less noticeable recoil. This can be an advantage in as much as they reduce the fatigue the shooter might experience in shooting a number of targets in fairly quick succession. It is sometimes the case, however, that semi-automatics are temperamental when the brand of ammunition normally and successfully used is changed. Jams in feeding or extracting ammunition may occur which can be very distracting. These problems can usually be overcome by ensuring you have a sufficient supply of the ammunition your gun prefers. Moreover, the regular user of a semi-automatic will almost certainly develop the habit of becoming quite fastidious in stripping and cleaning his gun at regular intervals; this will ensure that the many moving parts in the gun continue to work and can be replaced if they have broken.

Over-and-unders are less prone to problems induced by changes in ammunition brands, to the point where the topic is almost an irrelevance. The better guns of this type on the market are exceedingly reliable and require no more than normal cleaning and maintenance.

Over-and-unders and semi-automatics are more common on the skeet range than side-by-sides for two reasons. Firstly, the former types provide a view of the targets along a single sighting plane rather than along a rib either side of which is a barrel. Secondly, side-by-sides tend to be, on average, at least a pound lighter in weight than the other types which has the effect of increasing the perceived recoil felt.

Some will argue that the view down a side-by-side introduces a greater degree of pointability than that offered by the single-sighting plane, and under some lighting and background conditions I would not argue with this. On balance, however, I am persuaded through experience that a gun with a single-sighting plane is easier to point for the purpose of hitting the maximum number of skeet targets.

A typical gun for Olympic skeet will weigh between 7½lb and 8¼lb. An over-and-under for this sport will normally have 28in barrels while an equivalent semi-automatic will have a 26in barrel.

Since the majority of targets will be no more than about 25 yards distant when they are shot, little if any choke is required for the pattern at this range to be sufficiently dense to ensure a hit provided the target is actually in the pattern. Some skeet guns have what are called retro or trumpet chokes, where the internal diameter of the barrel in the area of the choke is bigger than the nominal bore size. The effect of a retro choke is to produce a slightly longer shot string than would otherwise be the case. Some argue that this is an advantage, though whether it is or not depends on your interest in theoretical issues. Many shooters perform successfully at the highest levels without retro chokes, so you may conclude that it is a matter of choice as to whether you really need them .

Most over-and-under users prefer guns fitted with a single trigger, and the vast majority of such guns are only available in this configuration these days. However, that is not to say that an over-and-under with double triggers is unsuitable, far from it. The renowned former Soviet shooter, Tomas Imnaishvilli, used a double trigger gun for many years to good effect, winning many international championships including the 1981 World Championship with 198 x 200.

Arguably the most important part of a skeet gun is the stock. As already mentioned, in Olympic skeet the gun butt must be held in contact with the hip-bone until a target emerges from the trap-house. When the target comes into view, the gun must be such that it can be brought to a firing position in the shoulder and aligned with the target *with the minimum of inconvenience*. This requires the stock to be the 'right' shape to suit the user: let us consider for a few moments, what this means.

To say that gun stocks come in all shapes and sizes is a truism and an understatement. It is most unusual for two gun stocks to be the same unless a gunmaker has deliberately set out with this in mind—even mass-produced guns vary. In order to suit any one person, it is important that the stock is the correct length, so that he or she can mount the gun comfortably without his nose being hit by his trigger hand when the gun is fired. Shooters new to Olympic skeet often make the mistake of using a gun with too short a stock in the false belief that this will make the task of mounting the gun that much easier. In fact in most cases, a *longer* stock will lead to better results. Most guns for Olympic skeet have stocks which provide a length of pull of between 14¼in and 14¾in, and unless you are particularly larger or smaller than average, you should anticipate your correct stock length to be in this range.

The drops at the point of the comb and heel need to be such that, when the gun is mounted, your sighting eye can just see the entire rib. This will enable you to place the shot at the correct vertical height relative to your point of aim. The majority of skeet targets are shot at when they are either travelling near enough horizontally or actually falling. It is therefore important that the gun shoots to the point of aim, and neither excessively high nor low of this—a high- or a low-shooting gun for Olympic skeet is a positive disadvantage. The usual measurements for the drops at the point of the comb and heel for guns suitable for Olympic skeet are around 1½in and 2¼in respectively.

The amount of cast-off or cast-on of the stock, normally for a right- or left-handed shooter respectively, must be correct so that your shots are placed in the correct lateral position relative to your point of aim. A right-handed shooter will find that he will shoot to the right of his targets if his gun has more cast-off than he requires. It is normal for Olympic skeet guns to have some cast, but the amount is 'slight'.

The pitch of the stock refers to the angle the butt plate makes relative to a line along the top rib. To establish pitch, close your gun and stand it upright with the butt plate resting evenly on a flat horizontal surface; place a vertical straightedge against the top of the standing breech and measure the distance between the straightedge and the top rib at the muzzle end. Typical measurements for Olympic skeet guns will be between 1½in and 3in, though to a great extent the amount of pitch you require is governed by comfort factors. However, if the pitch is too great, you will find the muzzles of the gun have a tendency to drop as you mount, causing you to shoot low. Conversely if the pitch is too little, you will tend to shoot too high, and in extreme cases you may also experience discomfort if the toe of the stock digs into you.

In the same way that it is only possible for a tailor to fit a suit to a person when he is present, it is not possible for you to have a gun fitted unless you visit a reliable shooting instructor. Money spent in this exercise will most probably save you far more in the long run, and your progress and enjoyment will be far greater.

You will find that most guns for skeet have pistol or half-pistol grip stocks these days; it is a matter of personal preference which you choose.

You may also see some skeet shooters using guns with Monte Carlo stocks with combs parallel to the line of the barrels. The theory behind the

The gun comes into the shoulder as the target moves towards the 'killing' area

111

use of such stocks is that they always allow the shooter to mount his gun so that the sighting eye is at the appropriate height relative to the top rib, regardless of whether the gun has been mounted correctly or not. While this argument has merit, it must be said that there is at least an equally strong argument for learning to mount the gun correctly in the first place. It would not be doing the student of Olympic skeet a favour to suggest the adoption of 'short-cut' measures before he has learned the basics of the game.

Ammunition

Having discussed the attributes of a suitable gun and the importance of gun-fit, the ammunition which you will use for Olympic skeet is worthy of mention. In competition, the maximum load of shot which is currently permitted weighs 24g (it was reduced from 28g on January 1 1993). Previously the maximum shot size allowable was 2.0mm diameter, which equates to No 9 shot size in English nomenclature. But the new rules allow the shot size to be optionally increased to 2.5mm diameter, roughly English No 6 shot size.

A reasonably fast cartridge is generally accepted as being required for Olympic skeet, and there are many suitable brands on the market to choose from which fall into this category. However, it would be incorrect to assume that high velocity on its own is the principal requirement of a suitable cartridge. There is a tendency for recoil to increase as velocity increases and this is unhelpful, especially where a newcomer to the sport has not fully mastered the technique of consistent gun-mounting, the inevitable result being discomfort leading to many related shooting ills. More important in ammunition is reliability and consistency through the use of good quality components and loading techniques, so that variation in ballistic performance, pattern quality and penetration is at a minimum. As in life in general, you normally get what you pay for; but that said, you certainly do not need to buy the dearest on offer to obtain the quality capable of performing at the highest levels.

Other equipment

Absolutely vital pieces of equipment for Olympic skeet, in common with all other shooting disciplines, are hearing protectors and shooting glasses.

Well-fitting headphones are generally accepted as offering greater protection than ear plugs. An investment of but a few pounds can thus reduce the prospect of suffering from incurable hearing loss or even worse, tinitus.

Shooting glasses should always be worn, whether you require them in prescription form or not, to protect the eyes from fragments of broken targets, ricocheting pellets and, when using a semi-automatic, the hot gases and other debris which can sometimes be emitted from the ejection port. The lenses should be toughened, and plastic is usually recommended in preference to glass.

Even if normally you have no need to wear glasses, you will find that wearing them for shooting brings certain benefits which may not be immediately obvious. In the majority of Olympic skeet competitions these days, both at home and abroad, the targets are coloured red or orange and some people find that shooting in glasses which have tinted lenses is an advantage because they can see these targets more clearly against the varied backgrounds which shooting ranges offer than would otherwise be the case. Depending on personal preference and conditions, the tints might vary from pink to red, violet to blue, or green to grey. There is no need for more than one pair of shooting glasses initially—that would be an expensive exercise; but it is important that you do take appropriate precautions.

Basic Technique

So, having now reached the stage where we have considered the equipment, it is time to start using it!

Holding the gun

We have already stressed the importance of gun-fit, but exactly how should you hold your gun? For ease of explanation we will consider here the case of a right-handed shooter.

The job of the left hand is to support the forward weight of the gun and to contribute significantly in pointing the gun. The left hand should therefore be positioned on the fore-end in a way which is helpful in achieving both tasks economically. The fore-end should be grasped so the weight it supports falls diagonally across the palm from the base of the forefinger. The fingers should be on the right side of the fore-end and the thumb should be on the left side. The gripping pressure exerted by the fingers and thumb should be firm but not tight.

The easiest way to convey the idea of the firmness needed is to think of the grip which you would use to hold a handful of eggs: too tight and the eggs would break, too loose and they might be dropped! It is important for the grip to be relaxed so as to avoid tension, which would otherwise have the effect of inhibiting the free movement of the wrist and arm as the gun is mounted and pointed.

The right hand is used to support the weight of the rearward part of the gun and, in unison with the left hand, controls the mounting of the stock to the face and shoulder.

Assuming the gun has a pistol or half-pistol grip, the right hand should be positioned near the base of the grip so that the first joint of the trigger finger can comfortably reach the blade of the trigger while the other fingers are curled around the grip. The thumb should be wrapped over and around the top of the grip so that it points to, or is just in contact with the second finger.

Right-hand grip pressure, as in the case of the left-hand grip, should be firm but not rigidly tight, for the same reasons as before.

The correct stance

Having discussed how to hold the gun, we should consider the correct stance to adopt before we discuss the mechanics of gun-mounting. First let us deal with the foot positions.

Imagine you are standing at the centre of a huge, horizontal clockface, and that your target is at the 12 o'clock position. To position yourself so as to shoot at this target comfortably, place your left foot so that it points towards 1 o'clock, and your right foot so that it points towards 3 o'clock, with a line across the tips of the toes of both feet pointing towards 11 o'clock. The distance between the inside of your heels should be about nine inches. This geometry is one which can be used to shoot all the targets in Olympic skeet, the orientation being one of your choosing—that is, where you intend to shoot at the target, which will be your 12 o'clock reference point.

To place the body in the correct position, adopt the foot position just described and stand normally upright with your weight slightly favouring your left foot. Your weight should be on the balls of your feet, not on the heels, but the soles of both feet should be in contact with the ground.

Now imagine that you have a straight tent-pole running down your left side passing through your body from the top of your left shoulder, down your torso and left leg to the ground, where it emerges from your foot. The imaginary tent-pole should be kept vertical except for being inclined slightly towards the 12 o'clock position throughout all movements associated with gun-mounting and firing.

The importance of our tent-pole is that it is the line about which the upper body will rotate, either from the left or right as required, as the gun is swung horizontally to intercept a target. A lack of application of this principle results in a tendency for the muzzles of the gun to describe a rainbow arc as they are swung, leading to shooting under some targets.

Mounting the gun

Gun-mounting is the act of bringing the gun from the ready position to the firing position, and is arguably the most important single aspect in learning to shoot Olympic skeet successfully; in fact the mechanics of gun-mounting are relatively simple to master once you have become familiar with the stance, body position and grip of your gun.

As stated at the outset, in Olympic skeet the rules dictate that you must hold your gun with a part of the butt in contact with your hip-bone when calling for a target. The task now is to learn how to bring the gun from this position to a firing position in a timely way which provides you with the best opportunity to shoot with consistent accuracy and comfort. Let us use the shooting of the low-house target from station 7 as an example to explain the gun-mounting technique.

**Olympic skeet calls for perfect gun mounting on each and every target.
This makes it excellent training also for other disciplines**

The chosen target should be broken at a point in its flight in the vicinity of the target crossing point. Let this point be our 12 o'clock position for this target. The feet will be positioned on the shooting station as described earlier.

With the gun held correctly in both hands, the toe of the butt touching the hip-bone, elevate the muzzles until they are set at a height directly over the target crossing point where the target, when released, will fly into view.

Call for the target, but do not move until you see it clearly over your muzzles. Then, using predominantly the left hand, gently push the muzzles into the target and keep them so aligned as, using the right hand, you raise the stock to the face and shoulder. When the shoulder is brought into firm contact with the butt plate, your right eye will be looking straight along the rib at the target: at that instant, without further adjustment, you can pull the trigger and watch the target break.

The gentle push towards the target is important: not only does it provide room for the stock to be raised smoothly to the face, it is also the initiation of a progressive weight transfer to the left foot which places the body in a position to better absorb recoil and, more significantly for crossing and quartering targets, frees the body to rotate to the left or right about the line previously represented by our imaginary tent-pole.

The perfection of the gun-mount requires a considerable amount of practice. This is best accomplished not on a skeet range firing costly ammunition, but with an unloaded gun in the convenience of your home in front of a large mirror. Practice this way in slow motion will teach you the feel of the correct movements which you can visually check until you are satisfied you have mastered the technique.

A common fault is to allow the muzzles to drop below the target as the stock is raised, which then necessitates a further corrective movement by the left hand to realign the muzzles on the target. This additional movement is obviously not only a waste of precious time, it introduces the chances of aiming the shotgun like a rifle, a fatal error in all types of shotgun shooting.

Before we consider how to shoot a complete round of Olympic skeet station by station, we should discuss the two different methods of hitting crossing or quartering targets, as understood in skeet-shooting circles: these are usually called the 'swing-through' and the 'maintained lead' methods.

In order to put the shot charge in the right place to hit a crossing target it is necessary to have the shotgun pointing ahead of it by an appropriate amount at the instant of firing. The swing-through and maintained-lead methods both seek to achieve this, but by different means.

The swing-through and maintained-lead methods

It is likely that you are already familiar with the swing-through method, particularly if you learned your shooting at game or rough shooting or at sporting clays. It is often considered to be the traditional method of shooting, and involves bringing the gun from a position behind the target to a position ahead of it, firing either when the appropriate sight picture is established or relying on the speed of the swing to place the shot in the right place as the target is passed.

With the maintained-lead method, the gun is kept ahead of the target at all times. The appropriate lead or forward allowance is applied by the shooter as the gun is mounted through reference to the relative positions of the moving target and the muzzles of the gun. The act of pulling the trigger takes place the instant the gun is mounted.

While 'swing-through' is a good description of the first method because it conveys a readily understood impression of what actually takes place, 'maintained lead' is perhaps not so apt since it might be interpreted as being a studious and slow method involving tracking the target across the range. In fact, when put into practice by an experienced exponent of the technique, nothing could be further from the truth. The essence of maintained-lead shooting is that because the gun is only travelling at the speed of the target and the time taken to mount it to a firing position is used to establish the correct forward allowance, many experienced maintained-lead shooters will kill their targets more quickly and reliably than their swing-through counterparts.

Whether you employ one method or the other is largely a matter of personal choice. While both methods can be used successfully, as you gain confidence you will begin to appreciate why the majority of Olympic skeet shooters use the maintained-lead method. That said, even experienced maintained-lead shooters are forced to use the swing-through method for the second targets of doubles, because the sheer speed of the targets in Olympic skeet dictates that the gun will start from a position behind the second target of a pair after the first target has been shot.

It is also true that, on occasions, even an experienced maintained-lead shooter will be caught out by not reacting as he would have liked, and will be forced to shoot the odd target using the swing-through method. You might be drawn to conclude that this confers an advantage for the maintained-lead exponent in that he has this second string to his bow, and it is difficult to argue against this.

Shooting A Complete Round

We shall now describe how to shoot a complete round of Olympic skeet, target by target, using the maintained-lead method where appropriate.

Station 1

On station 1 you will be required to shoot a single high-house target followed by a double. The first target of any round is important—in the words of Joe Neville, the Great Britain team coach, it is a 'big-shot' because once hit, it constitutes a confidence-builder and provides you with the foundation for a good round. If missed, you will be struggling all the way home to make 24 x 25!

To shoot the high-house target, first identify where you intend to hit it; this should be just before the target crossing point. Using this as your reference point to identify your notional 12 o'clock position, align your feet and body as previously described relative to this point.

With one cartridge in your gun, take up the ready position with the butt in contact with your hip-bone and the muzzles elevated about 45° from the horizontal. Look at an area in space about 20° above your muzzles, prepare yourself to respond to the *sight* of the target, and call for it to be released.

It is very important to train yourself to respond only to the sight of the target and not to the noise of the trap releasing it if you hope to develop a reliable technique. Many strange noises emanate from trap-houses at times which are quite distracting, but nevertheless, they have to be ignored.

When the target comes into view, push the gun muzzles into it with the left hand and, keeping that relationship, raise the stock to the face pulling the trigger the instant the stock is supported by the shoulder. The result should be one powdered target.

The first shot of the double should be executed in precisely the same manner, but after shooting it, you will need to look for the second target which you will see fast approaching you to the left of your muzzles. Without taking your head from the stock, you will swing smoothly past this until you 'see' a lead of about one foot when you will pull the trigger again and watch it break some ten yards away.

Station 2

Having successfully negotiated station 1, proceed to station 2 where you will shoot a single target from each trap followed by a double. You should be aware that the rules of Olympic skeet require you to load two cartridges when shooting singles at all stations, with the exception of stations 1 and 8 where only one cartridge can be loaded at a time.

You will shoot the single high-house target first, and should try to hit it just before it reaches the target crossing point. As before, this then becomes your 12 o'clock reference position to enable you to set your feet and stance accordingly. With the gun butt in contact with the hip-bone, turn the upper body from the waist so that the gun muzzles point at a spot along the target's flight-path about ten yards out from the trap-house. Turn your head slightly to the left and look at an area in space between the muzzles and the trap-house where you expect to see the target when it emerges. Remain still and alert and call for the target.

When you first see the target, because it is fairly close to you and is travelling at speed, it may appear as a blur. You will need to focus on it quickly. Just before it reaches the position of your stationary gun muzzles and there is an imminent danger that it will pass them, start your gun-mounting movements.

The left hand will start its forward push movement to align the muzzles with the target, the upper body will start to rotate to the right to keep the muzzles just ahead, the right hand will start to raise the stock to the face. These motions will be smooth and continuous.

While this is going on, the distance between the target and the muzzles is being monitored by the brain as the mounting takes place; through reference to 'sight pictures' which have been learned through practice, the gun-mount will be completed when the correct picture is seen. At that instant the trigger will be pulled while the muzzles are kept moving along the target's flight-path.

The sight picture needed to hit this target will depend on your personal reaction time. As a guide, however, you should expect to see a lead of about 18 inches.

The low-house target on station 2 is comparatively easy. You will shoot it approximately halfway between the target crossing point and the high house, your new 12 o'clock reference position, after it has traversed the majority of the range.

Adopt the gun-down ready position relative to the reference position, rotate the upper body so that the muzzles are on the intended target flight-path, some ten yards out from the low house. Look for the target to appear between the muzzles and the trap-house, and call for the target.

When the target emerges, let it come to your muzzles and then begin your mounting movement, the left hand controlling the gun-point which should be just ahead of the target, the upper body rotating to the left as the right hand raises the butt to the face.

Once again, the brain will monitor the sight picture as the mounting takes place with the movement being completed when the picture is correct. The instantaneous pulling of the trigger while the muzzles are kept moving will ensure a hit. The lead needed to break this target will depend upon your reaction time, but will be around 2½ feet.

You should approach hitting the double on station 2 as if you are setting out to shoot the two single targets. The high-house target must be shot first, so the feet and body should be orientated as before for that shot. After you have shot the first target you will need to look for the one from the low house. This will by now be slightly to the left of your muzzles, which will require you to reverse your swing and pass it to obtain the lead needed to break it.

In order to reduce Olympic skeet to its simplest level you should try to shoot all the single targets where you will shoot the targets in the doubles. This will keep to a minimum the different sight pictures the brain will have to memorise.

Station 3

The shooting format at station 3 is identical to that at station 2. Having moved around the range further from the high house, however, both high- and low-house targets will appear more as crossing than quartering shots and consequently will require as much as two feet more lead. That said, the shooting technique to use will be just as before, and the targets will be shot in more or less the same places along their flight-paths.

You may find that at the ready position you need to point your muzzles a yard or so further out from the trap-houses than on station 2 to avoid the targets getting past your muzzles before you have reacted to them. This adjustment is one which you will only determine through a certain amount of trial and error.

Station 4

Station 4 is at the mid-point of the skeet circle equidistant from the trap-houses, and you will be required to shoot a single target from the high and low houses in turn. Both targets are treated as full crossing shots.

The high-house target should be shot over or slightly to the left of the target crossing point; there is no particular merit in trying to shoot this target early in its flight. Fast shooting may look spectacular but it is better to shoot at a pace which suits you to ensure maximum consistency.

As on previous stations, where you decide to shoot the target becomes your reference point, so you can set your feet and body position. In the gun-down ready position the muzzles should be placed about ten yards out from the high house on the target flight-path. The target will be shot in the same manner as described before, and will require you to see a lead of about five feet.

The technique for shooting the low-house target is the same as for the high-house one, in mirror-image form. It is important to point out, however,

Jim Sheffield shooting at a low-house target at the optimum point

that the two targets differ in trajectory since the high-house trap is ten feet above the ground compared with the low-house machine's three feet. The consequence of this is, that all low-house targets rise more steeply on their flight to the target crossing point than their counterparts from the high house. Therefore, when tackling the station 4 low-house target, ensure that your shot is high enough to take account of the target's rising flight.

Station 5

On station 5, moving round towards the low house on the range, you will be faced with shooting a single high-house target followed by one from the low house and then a double, where the low-house target must be taken first.

The technique to be applied for all these shots and the leads associated with them have already been learned, because the targets at this station are the near mirror-image of those on station 3. As in the case of the station 4 low-house target, you will need to recognise that the low-house target on station 5 rises to the target crossing point, and to make appropriate allowance for this. You may also find, especially when shooting the double if you have shot the first target a little slowly, that the high-house target is dropping at the point where you will shoot it; in this case, you will need to shoot slightly under this target.

Most right-handed shooters, whether experienced or novice, find the double on station 5 the hardest in a round of skeet. This is not only because of the speed and trajectory of the second target, but more significantly

Mike Reynolds: note how his eyes are fixed onto the target as the gun is mounted into the shoulder and cheek

Ed Scherer advocates shooting English skeet with the maintained lead method

Left: Roger Silcox watching the target over the muzzles as he mounts the gun

Jim Sheffield shooting Olympic skeet, gun well out of the shoulder and weight on the front foot because all right-handed shooters experience greater difficulty maintaining the correct body posture when rotating to their right.

A shooter who lacks the subtleness to rotate the upper body sufficiently, may tend to use the hands and arms to move the muzzles sideways into an 'apparently' correct sighting position, with the result that the stock is pulled away from the face. This loss of contact leads to a catastrophic pointing error, the target usually being missed by a wide margin.

Station 6

Having identified the similarities between station 5 and station 3, it will be no great surprise to learn that the shots at station 6 are likewise nearly mirror-images of those at station 2. Once again you will be faced with singles and a double, to be shot in precisely the same format as at station 5, and you should use the same technique and leads as discussed for station 2.

Station 7

On station 7, immediately in front of the low house, you will shoot only a double; the low-house target flies directly away from you and this is taken first. This double is without doubt the easiest in a round of skeet, but it is surprising how often the low-house target is missed, even on occasions by very experienced shooters. This can happen if you fail to pick up its line of flight properly, which can result in shooting to one side or the other. It is more often missed in windy conditions when it is prone to rise or fall as the shot is committed, leading to a miss under or above it.

As on station 1, it is essential to react to the sight of the target and not to the sound of the trap; any movement of gun or body before the target emerges normally results in a miss. Therefore when waiting for the target it is vital to remain still.

Station 8

The last station, number 8, is at the mid-point between the trap-houses; it is well known as the one where competitions have been won and lost. You will be required to shoot a single target from each house, starting with the high house. In each case if the targets are to be counted, they must be hit before they pass a line from station 4 to station 8.

It is true that there is not a great deal of time to shoot either target before it becomes 'out of bounds'. An intense amount of concentration is required to see the targets early in their flight, and to carry out the smooth gun-mounting that is needed to bring the gun to the face with the muzzles pointing in the right direction. Great demands are therefore placed on proper technique; but when this is applied by an experienced shooter, the targets can be broken with apparent ease well before they reach the shooter.

When shooting the high-house target, select a spot in front of you along the target's flight-path where you intend to fire. Aligning your feet and body with respect to this, as for all previous shots, place the gun muzzles about a yard to the right of the target opening at a height where the target will fly. Look for the target at the point where you will first see it emerging directly from the trap-house opening. Call for the target, and on *no* account move until you see it. When it comes into view, place the muzzles onto it and keep them so pointed as you mount and fire. If you have correctly coordinated your movements, the result will be a satisfying ball of smoke ahead of you.

The low-house target is approached in the same manner, remembering that it is the near mirror-image of the high-house shot.

Olympic Skeet Competitions

Major Olympic skeet competitions at home and abroad are normally shot over a course of 200 targets per competitor. This means that our description of what takes place during one round of 25 targets is repeated eight times, usually over a two- or three-day period. Club-level competitions in this country are frequently over 50, 75 or 100 targets, which provides a flavour of the bigger events without the time and expense otherwise involved.

If, once you have tried Olympic skeet, you develop aspirations to take it up more seriously, you would be advised to obtain proper instruction from a coach with specific knowledge and experience of the discipline. This will save you much frustration and money in the long run, even though the initial outlay for lessons might seem high.

Once you become fairly proficient at Olympic skeet, and if you are competitive by nature, you may become drawn into taking part in CPSA registered competitions. And having gained some experience and maybe success at these, you may wish to enter competitions held specifically about six times each year to select individuals and teams to represent Great Britain at international events.

Being selected to represent Great Britain in events at home and abroad, where your skills will be pitted against those of the best shooters from other countries, is a proud moment indeed. It will give you the opportunity to see the very best shooters in action, to experience competition at the highest levels, and if you are observant, to learn a great deal in the process, as well as making new friends.

Over the years the competitors from Eastern Europe and the former Soviet Union have tended to dominate international events. They continue to treat the sport very seriously, leaving little to chance in the way of physical and mental preparation and team organisation. Their approach is nothing short of professional through and through.

This country has lacked the funding and resources, perhaps even the will, to compete on similar terms. That said, while we arguably have not had the backing we deserve, on occasions our competitors have achieved some notable results. Dave Seabrook, for example, won the bronze medal as long ago as 1973 in the World Championships in Australia behind two Soviet competitors. Wally Sykes shot-off for the bronze medal in the 1983 World Championships in Canada, and Paul Bentley shot-off for the silver medal in the 1985 World Championships in Italy. Our most consistent international performer over very many years, Joe Neville, came fourth in the Olympic Games in 1972. Perhaps you, if you are sufficiently dedicated, motivated and talented, can aspire to even greater things.

As happens every few years, the rules for Olympic skeet are once again in the throes of change. From 1 January 1993, the maximum permissible shot load will be reduced to 24g and the format for a round of skeet will be altered. Gone will be the single low-house target on station 2 and, likewise, the single high-house target on station 6. Instead, an additional pair will be shot on station 4 after the two single targets on that station have been shot.

Without doubt these changes will make the game somewhat harder, but you can be sure that those who can shoot will continue to produce the scores which will win; do not, therefore, let these changes affect your resolve for excellence.

Jim Sheffield first made the British Olympic skeet team in 1980, having previously been four-times English Skeet Champion. He has since won both the British and English titles at Olympic skeet, plus the Grand Prix of Europe (where he completed 200 straight) and the Grand Prix of Lopik.

6

Trap Disciplines:

DTL, ABT, UT, OT

Andrew Perkins

Andrew Perkins

Trap shooting can offer some of the most elusive and satisfying experiences available to the clay pigeon shooter. It can also be the number one humiliator! Since the late 1850s when sparrow and pigeon 'trap' shooting was becoming popular, the methods and options have changed considerably. Initially the birds were placed under upturned flowerpots with long strings attached. Soon after, collapsing boxes were developing which were there one second and flat the next, thus making the task far harder as little indication was given as to which box was going to produce the target out of however many were used.

Further developed versions of the above are still in use in some countries today, and provide the chance to win or lose large sums of money. Despite the use of sophisticated electronic machines, chance still plays a significant part in the outcome. No matter how skilled the competitors, the challenge facing each one is not identical—one may have birds flying in directions he finds manageable, whereas another's may just happen to fly to quarters he finds difficult, the balance of angles not being the same for each competitor.

To add even more complexity, human pigeon throwers are sometimes employed, and the pigeon's flight can be influenced in unpredictable ways by several different methods.

Other forms of target were also used in the middle of the last century, among them glass balls stuffed with feathers and projected into the sky with cart springs. The targets were very predictable—they also caused major problems cleaning up afterwards. 'Bent' steel propeller blades spun and projected from launchers also enjoyed a brief period of use. However, not until the advent of the so-called clay pigeon did the disciplines we know today have any chance to evolve; the new target opened up many possibilities unthought of before. Consistent speed and direction were obtainable, so trap technology also began to evolve apace. Nowadays we have fully automatic throwing machines available which can be computer controlled. This complexity means that sophisticated competitive target sequences can be thrown, as well as repeated targets for 'no bird' problems; it is the ultimate in making competitions as even as possible for all the shooters. Bear in mind, however, that in the British Isles the climatic conditions, especially the light and wind, vary enormously in short periods of time, making totally even competition less likely than in some other countries.

Trap shooting has developed to include a number of disciplines which are now grouped within the term. Not in any particular order, they include names such as Down The Line, American Trap, Handicap Single Barrel, Nordic, Handicap by Distance, Wobble, Automatic Ball Trap, Universal and Olympic Trench, Double Rise and ZZ. Which is the easiest, the most fun, or the hardest to shoot? All a matter of individual viewpoint!

I am convinced that the faster trap disciplines provide the most difficult targets available, and that under some adverse conditions the task can be significantly beyond that envisaged when the challenge was laid down. Because you are presented with an unknown, fast-receding, edge-on target producing a minimum profile with round hard edges and usually changing its pitch and bank angles, the response required to connect your shot charge with said target is very precise indeed!

Keith Bond is one of the UK's most consistent DTL shooters

There was a time when live pigeons were shot with side-by-side guns. These were made by several of the top London makers and evolved very quickly due to the demands of the clients who were competing often and amassing experience quickly. Their specifications included barrels which were usually long, heavier than normal, and with prominent ribs; Monte Carlo stocks, and a beaver-tail fore-end; and a single trigger associated with a Prince of Wales type grip. Analysing the aforementioned changes to the side-by-side English game gun, you will appreciate that radical modifications were involved. The weight increased as did the manageable pointability. It is interesting to me that great attention was paid to the distribution of the overall weight.

The beaver-tail fore-end provided much needed control for the lead hand, at the same time allowing better visibility between the thumb and fingers as the grip was far wider and lower than before. Stability was also enhanced by weight increase in this area. Various degrees of pistol grip enabled a more consistent single trigger location, consequently contributing to a more precise control. The sum combination of changes to the specifications brought about a quite different gun, much more successful for the task at hand. Today we have a veritable array of guns described as trap, interestingly nearly all over-and-under configuration. However, in the same way that a racing car may look the same as another, the make-up of it can be totally dissimilar to the winning car. One of the aspects of shooting is that you are reliant on only yourself when in action. There is no telemetry, intercoms, or associated umbilicals in play. The relationship between detail specification, fitting, handling, and the associated feel of the gun to user

Good visibility and a well-kept ground: Belvoir SG

(assuming the configuration is appropriate to the discipline) is the secret to successful shooting.

So why is it so difficult to hit the targets consistently and achieve high scores? Some shooters do. The top hot shots play a different game to most other competitors. They have shot literally thousands and thousands of cartridges over the years, so their timing and precision, governed by their gun-fit/cartridge/choke combination, together with their stance, balance and consistent mount and well-disciplined technique, are all second nature to them. Theirs is no longer an interrogation of the target; it is instant recognition of the situation and job done.

As in most sports, another viewpoint is often needed to keep a keen competitor on the road to success. Those important combinations are not as easy to analyse on your own and this is where I often find the most satisfaction in my days at work. It is usually a plateauing or drop in scores that brings most serious clients for a lesson. Depending on the problem to solve, I usually follow closely the mental check-list of causes and effects. Are both the stance and the balance sound? What cartridge/choke combinations is used? And, maybe the gun is never going to really suit the individual?

For those of you who might like to check your own stance and balance, there is a simple yet quite useful exercise to try. With weight slightly forward on the feet, mount the gun (unloaded!) virtually parallel to the ground pointing straight ahead. Now swing approximately 50° left, then back through centre and 50° right and back to centre, and 50° up, and finally depress the 'line' below the horizontal. Did you feel that your balance was still maintained at the limit of each swing? If not, move your feet to allow the exercise to be performed more comfortably. Undue strain on your back calls for immediate change to avoid problems later on.

As with most things that are done properly and stand the test of time, good foundations in shooting are vital. I am convinced that above everything else the final win or lose is very much influenced by the formative period. Keeping your technique simple, and maintaining that simplicity as you learn, will ensure those good habits, in the same way that proper mounting and good balance stay with you as you move from one discipline to the next, or progress to the top of any chosen disciplines.

Beware of self-correction, although it is obvious when explained, from a wrong turn taken. To give an example, if a fellow competitor has a succession of very good scores and is seen to be winning, there tends to be a lemming effect on the assumption that what works for him will work for you. Don't believe it: watch the top shots who have good solid styles, not the extremists who have succeeded in spite of themselves. As a rule, extreme styles are flawed, and sooner or later will fail to produce continually high scores.

It has to be recognised that there are certain basic targets which give great confidence, so that a competitor seems to think he'd have success without changing a thing, with any gun he picks up, and with virtually any cartridge. Yes, it certainly happens to some, for a while; but only if you establish yourself so firmly that you feel accomplished enough to start looking in detail, will you be able really to improve. And if the foundations of your shooting

Stepped rib guns are popular among some trap shooters

are flawed, then rebuilding those foundations can prove difficult, time-consuming, and expensive. I like to recommend to each client that a diary be kept of his practice as well as his competitions: details such as choke/cartridge combinations, in the analysis of success; first and second barrel shots and scores should be noted; gun dimensions and barrel plus fore-end weight, also stock and action weight; and any further additions should be weighed and recorded as well. Also, any other details which may significantly influence the optical or physical alignment need to be recorded.

Not too long ago I had a young Down The Line shooter come by for some

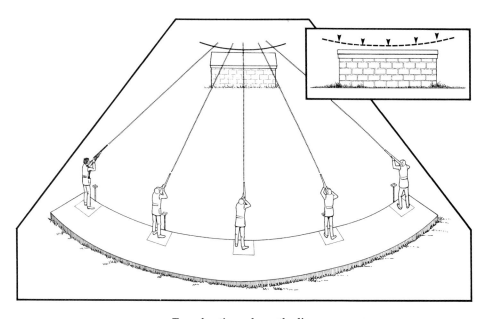

Trap shooting – down-the-line

help. He had been shooting 97 x 100 DTL scores so had decided to progress to Automatic Ball Trap. Disappointed he could do no better than 18 x 25 (and that was lucky), we set about to sort out the difference. DTL is far more manageable than ABT due to the shorter flight distance, narrower angles, and because the throwing height is constant. This individual's success at DTL was determined by his second barrel. He was not a good first-barrel shot on DTL, so the speed of the targets of ball trap seemed unconquerable. He had made the transition too soon, as his quick responses and good eyesight had lulled him into a false security with the slower consistent targets of DTL.

A squad of trap shooters will look to establish a rhythm.
Note how this shooter has really got into the target

Having asked him to mount a pre-checked empty gun, it was very obvious that a fair percentage of his problem was due to a less-than-perfect gun-fit. A visit to the pattern plates confirmed that not only was the stock too long and too straight, but also too broad and so hitting him in the face; further, the point of impact was well high left. Balance, too, relies very much on gun-fit, and in consequence this man's balance was all wrong. The long straight stock was encouraging an English longbow stance, with body and feet perpendicular to the gun, making it virtually impossible for him to swing the gun left or right whilst keeping balance. His weight was back on his heels. Obviously the gun-fit had to be corrected first, and I suggested an inch and a half be taken off the stock. His trigger hand was far too great a distance from his nose, and his left hand was holding the gun at the action rather than the fore-end. We reduced the thickness of the top of the stock (by careful attention to detail shaping) which solved the high left impact point. The stance was then easily corrected: I suggested 7 minutes past 12 with the left foot and 10 minutes past twelve with the right foot and heels off-set.

As a result of all of the above efforts, the combination immediately improved the DTL first barrel hits, making his transition to ABT far more encouraging.

Creating your own luck may seem an unusual thought, but it is instrumental in many win or lose situations. Make a point of shooting at venues which have a reputation for consistent regulation targets that do actually break when hit at the right range. Knowing you have hit a target but not having it break, is totally disastrous to a novice and horribly confusing to the experienced shot. There is far too little attention to this sort of detail paid by some operators of shooting grounds, and certainly bad targets— whether due to erratic release timing or wrong distances or angles—have an extremely negative effect on one's scores. Confidence is likely to be destroyed, and it takes some recovering. The clay pigeon manufacturer should be known so that appropriate choke and cartridge selection can be made, as some brands are far harder to break than others.

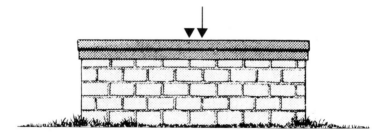

When shooting peg 3, right-handers should try starting with their gun just right of centre above the traphouse

Personally I do not recommend watching other people's targets to any great extent. If you do, you'll have watched up to 150 per round instead of concentrating on the 25 of your own. Continuous target-watching serves little purpose, and can lead to impaired reactions when eventually your turn comes.

One problem experienced by many top trap-shooters is their orientation for different layouts. Sort out early on a stance which enables you to swing in the properly balanced manner described earlier. Having established the stance and associated weight distribution, relate it either to each stand position or to the target spread, paying regard to marker posts, lay of the land, and variable influences such as strong wind. Strong winds from any direction have considerable influence on the flight of targets. For example, if there is a gale-force wind from the left, favour your stand more to the right; moreover the birds going to the left will tend to climb much more than usual, and it is highly unlikely that there will be any straight targets. When waiting to shoot, know what is going on without watching every other target. Between shots balance your gun and relax your muscles as much as possible. Know the pace of the other shooters and don't get caught napping.

When your turn arrives, be mentally and physically ready to act; this is bound to lead to a more positive, confident routine reaction taking place.

Before you go to the line have everything ready. Check your clothing, your chokes, cartridges, glasses, blinkers, muffs and so on. Think about the wind speed and direction, the light; a change of anything at the last minute can really mess the result up. The competitor who does not do these simple things is by nature leaving a lot of variables around, and those very same variables will catch him out sooner or later. Maybe luck for you that he's caught unready or badly positioned, but more like an own goal for him.

Waterproofs are an essential accessory for all shooters, but particularly trap

Ask yourself if your inability to improve further follows any pattern. Can you hit every angled target within the scheme, given the knowledge of its flight path beforehand? And if not, why not? Chances are you are unable to cope with certain targets and/or certain shooting grounds. Take the individual angled problem targets first, maybe specifically the low, which is usually missed over the top or to its left or right; refer to the pattern plates again at the right range, make a clay-sized mark on them, and shoot several shots using your now established stance, same jacket and shoes as usual. It is very likely the pattern is not being directed where you would like it to be, or at best sometimes it is, sometimes not. And there comes a time when you must realise that skill alone does not win by itself: during your reaction to the target the dynamics of the gun do influence the angular changes it goes through; also optical reaction has directional control to a very fine degree,

Olympic trap targets are fast and fly at widely varying angles

Shooting DTL at Bywell Shooting Ground, Northumberland

and sometimes the one does not complement the other. For example, some barrel-heavy guns are described as 'steady' but in trap shooting or when handling unknown angle and variety speed targets, this very steadiness can prove to be a disadvantage. The initial line of departure from the trap-house is often not the same as that part of the target's flight where the shot charge is intended to connect with it. If the barrel has not realigned during the swing to the correct geometry to enable the shot charge to arrive at the right place in relation to the target, obviously it will miss.

Many people seem to think practice makes perfect, but in a lot of cases that is wrong and no amount of practice will provide top-class scores. You only have to look at motor racing or golf to see the difference that equipment makes—take this year's top driver, for example, and put him in another F1 car and probably he will not win to the same degree at all. Change the clubs of a top tournament player and he'll be in real trouble.

Guns vary immensely, even model to model. Once you have experimented and found a trap gun with which you have had an outright winning score in your class or overall (depending on the stage you have reached), keep it and don't change it or stop unless you have a very sound reason indeed to do so. Go to your trap club having arranged to have several guns to try, and do just that; you will be pleasantly surprised at how easy it is to shoot well with some, and how frustrating it is to shoot with others. And although they all may seem to you to fit, be aware that a lot of guns, especially in gun shops, feel that way! Get them in action, try before you buy, be aware of the differences, and the advantage can be yours.

DTL is a very good trap target on which to gain experience, even though you will hear it described as boring, pedestrian, and many other derogatory remarks. However, the fact remains that to score 100/300 takes a considerable amount of dedication, and to that end many people devote a great deal of time and energy—and still never get there! Beginners at trap shooting will find it quite hard enough, whilst at the same time they are

Olympic trap at North Wales Shooting School, near Chester

likely to connect with enough targets to allow them some modest feeling of confidence which usually adds fuel to the fire of determination for the future.

Guns of 30–32in barrel are about par for the course; the first barrel shoots a little high, the second is more line-of-sight, but accompanied by good crisp trigger pulls and a good gun-fit, it should score well. The trap-house, being an above-ground structure, seems to make the targets appear more manageable. When used, manual rather than acoustic release also allows more time in which to react. Many people who shoot DTL are very particular as to who is in their squad, due to the timing of the progress through the shots. Three-quarters and full choke serve as well as anything until you have good reason to use some other combination. Use good quality trap cartridge, no 8 first and maybe no 7 or no 7 1/2 second barrel.

ABT, UT and Olympic trap are sometimes difficult to separate in terms of challenge; at other times the differences are much more apparent. The random nature of the targets to each shooter in ABT is unique amongst these three disciplines: both UT and OT are computer controlled so that each competitor faces the same target angles, albeit wind and light can very much affect the competition. The heaviest-weight trap guns with long barrels are not so favoured for these disciplines—but beware the light, fast handling, 'feels fantastic in the gun shop' trap gun. These are inevitably hard to control consistently and usually contribute to erratic scores.

Borrow several guns and try the different handling combinations. Handling is extremely important in trap shooting, because once the initial move is made there is precious little time to change the reaction nature. Gun-fit is vital, and your ability to mount in the same place in the same way is essential to consistency. More choke than that required for DTL is usually

Lonato, in Northern Italy, where the trap ranges are superbly equipped

the form, although a lot depends on the conditions and your speed of response. Due to the percentage of targets which are either fast, or wide-angled, or edge-on and low, a very good pellet pattern is essential. Use good trap cartridges; anything less is false economy. Successful DTL, ABT, UT and OT shooting comes with dedication and sheer hard work; there is no single magic sentence to provide the winning formula.

A combination of progressively selected equipment, and precise use of the same in a trained reflex manner, produces the results. It is almost impossible to sequence a long run of shots from start to finish—in fact I find it difficult to analyse what *I'm* doing step by step whilst taking each shot. After the shot, however, various things may show as important: different-than-normal stance, weight distribution, hand-grip or whatever all need noting. Subtle changes contribute to the successful technique. Because the reactions are so spontaneous they have to be developed and fine-tuned to perfection. Scoring 49 out of 50 or 97 out of 100 at these disciplines feels easy when you've done it. Why? Mainly because everything goes quickly and directly, with usually very few second-barrel shots required. It is vital to feel that no particular target is a problem; a challenge they all are, but a problem—no way!

If you feel your chances of shooting a good score at a certain venue are decidedly less than at another, either sort out the reason why, or maybe you'll find those targets are well outside the discipline parameters—the choice is then usually yours. I do not feel that it is good news to part with your time or hard-earned money on some Mickey Mouse outfit's idea of the discipline. Any serious competitor will instantly appreciate properly presented targets to the discipline; neat and tidy surroundings promote matters still further. Efficiency is appreciated—the opposite is avoided.

Finally, a good ABT layout can be far harder than some of the UT or OT layouts which one encounters, though this needs qualifying on an individual basis, particularly as overall, the varying speeds of UT and OT contribute as much as anything to their rank in the average book! However, I do feel the top classifications start too low, and do not allow quite the subdivisions one might have expected. And in your progress up the ranks, the time will come when class-won places lose their appeal, and outright high gun position is the one to try for!

Andrew Perkins is an accomplished England international trap shooter and full-time shooting instructor with the Holland & Holland Shooting School.

ZZ Target Shooting

Pat Lynch

Pat Lynch

One of the least known but probably one of the most interesting forms of competitive shotgun shooting and one which is closest to the origins of the sport, is that of ZZ target, or to use its continental name, *Electrocibles*—translated literally this means 'electric target'. Recognised as being the fastest growing of all the shotgun shooting sports, it is now a major FITASC discipline controlled from Paris; it has had its own European Championships for the past twenty years, and since 1990 has also rated a World Championships.

Unlike clay shooting, which grew separately as a very inexpensive form of competitive shooting as compared to live birds, ZZ was designed specifically to replace the shooting of boxed pigeons in those countries where this particular sport had been banned. The requirement to produce a target which flew like a pigeon was quite a difficult problem, and the technology of plastics combined with the electrical engineering of the machines only came together in the late 1950s.

The original inventor was a Belgian, the chevalier David de Lossy, a very well known boxed pigeon shooter who in the 1950s recognised the fact that the days of pigeon shooting were limited. The sport had in fact finished in England in the 1910s through lack of interest and because of the high cost as compared with the clay pigeon, and in many European countries it was going the same way. David de Lossy began to experiment with propeller-shaped targets spun at high speed by an electric motor and released to fly. His first experiments involved the making of the target wings from zinc, and to give his project a name he used this word and the continental name of the Blue Rock live pigeon, the *Zurito*; thus the appellation ZZ found its way into the shooting vocabulary. Much work continued on the targets and launchers, carried out by de Lossy and his mechanic Fernand Moinil; the test site was the shooting club at Sart St Laurent in Belgium where the first competitions took place. These were usually a six-bird (Zurito) live pigeon shoot combined with a six-bird Zinc Zurito shoot.

In the early 1960s the project had progressed to a point where patents could be applied for: these were granted in France in 1962, and in England in 1963. The company began to produce the sets of five machines and the random control units, and also the targets, called *hélice* ('propeller', in English).

Thus a very brief history of the origin and development of the sport; however, to fully understand what ZZ shooting is all about, it is necessary to understand about boxed pigeon shooting. From the earliest days of

Olympic trap is the most demanding of the trap disciplines

ZZ targets must be shot before reaching the perimeter fence (the edge of the area of cut grass)

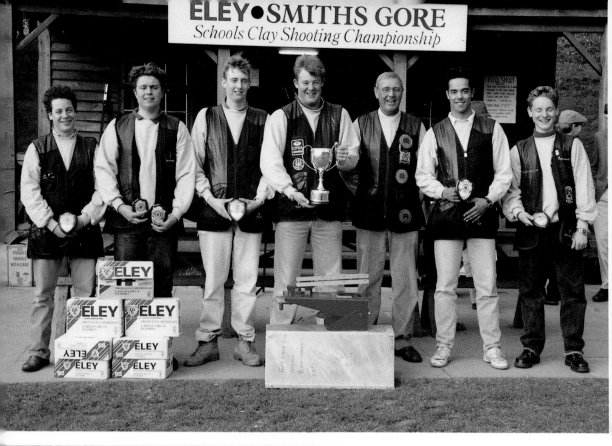

Sam Grice with his victorious Leys team in the Eley Smiths Gore Schools Championship

George Digweed: note how the gun is firmly mounted into the cheek, also the 'legs astride' stance

projectile weapons—sling shot and bows and arrows—there have always been competitions to see who was the best shot. As technology advanced, guns became a weapon of war, then a hunting tool and finally an item of sporting equipment. The development of the gun can definitely be linked to the requirements of the rich leisure shooter, and inextricably a part of this was the sport of bird shooting. This started with small birds under hats, which were 'pulled' off thus allowing the bird to fly; and progressed to the very sophisticated five-machine box system with electric release and compressed air-jets which are the norm today.

From about 1830, clubs were formed in most major European countries to hold competitions involving the shooting of pigeons released from boxes; the most important centre in Europe was England, and in particular London. At least half-a-dozen clubs were operating around London during the period 1860 to 1905, and shooting matches took place regularly, the prizes for which make today's rewards look very meagre by comparison. Sums of money in the region of £5,000 could be won by the top shot, and it was not unusual to find 'A shotgun by Messrs Purdey of London' on the prize list. Although the legal shooting of boxed pigeons ended in this country before World War I, it continued in most European countries up until the 1960s (in Monte Carlo, for instance) and the 1970s in Belgium, Germany and France. To this day it is still a very major shooting attraction in Spain, Portugal and Egypt, in many states in the USA, and all over Central and South America. However, the most famous pigeon-shooting country of all, Italy, has banned the sport from all public places and only private clubs carry it out now, on a very limited basis. Nevertheless, the sport is very much alive, and this year's World Championships in Malaga attracted an entry of 735 competitors; the first prize for just one of the six events was a cool 1m pesetas, that is £12,000!

One of the main attractions of this sport is the difficulty of shooting at a very fast, specially bred pigeon released from any one of five boxes; the other—and a major reason for the invention of ZZ to replace live pigeon shooting—is that of gambling, another of man's great passions. Organised and legal gambling takes place at every boxed pigeon shoot, and abroad at every major ZZ shoot, the sport being ideal gambling material due to the element of chance involved.

The rules of boxed pigeons shooting were formulated at the famous Gun Club, London in 1861, and further refined at the Hurlingham a few years later. The rules of ZZ shooting date only from the late 1960s and are identical in many ways to these original rules. Very briefly they are as follows: a flat area of ground is selected on which to erect a 2ft high close mesh fence in a half-circle, about 200ft across. In the centre of this half-ring are placed five special machines, some 15ft apart and facing towards the fence. There is a graduated walk-way placed exactly 25m behind the centre machine, going back in stages of 1m to a distance of 32m; the shooter stands on this at the appropriate mark (usually 25m, although handicapping can alter this). The five machines, each of which is exactly 21m from the fence, are loaded with a plastic target clipped on to the head of the machine. This loading is either carried out by a runner going to each machine, or by a trapper operating in a trench below the machines.

The shooter loads his gun and says 'Ready'. The person operating the buttons sets the electric motors of all the machines running and replies 'Ready'. The shooter then mounts his gun fully or partly as desired, and calls 'Pull'. The operator presses the release button, the random selection system causes a 12 x 18in steel flap on one of the machines to fall, and a target is instantly released. The target can go left or right, high or low, as the head of each machine is constantly tracking 90° left and right and at a speed which can be pre-set from 2,000rpm to 8,000rpm, dependent on wind conditions.

After release, the target accelerates and readjusts its flight several times like a gyroscope; it can make quite sharp turns according to the wind. The shooter is allowed two shots to 'kill' the target: this involves hitting it fairly centrally to dislodge the unbreakable white polythene centre cap (about the same size as a clay) from the wings and retaining ring which are made of a brittle orange plastic. The target must be broken quite quickly, whilst in its accelerating phase—you can't wait for the wings to stop revolving—so that the white centre drops within the perimeter fence. It is a 'loss' if the white centre falls outside the fence.

Having fired, the shooter ejects or unloads and walks off to be replaced by the next competitor; the machine in the meantime is loaded with another Hélice target, and on a prominent scoreboard the shooter is awarded a red disc for a kill or white for a loss.

A normal club competition would be held over 8 to 10 targets, a county or regional event over 15 targets, a national championships and European Championships over 20 targets, and the World Championships over 25 targets.

As already mentioned, the sport is controlled by FITASC, as is boxed pigeon shooting; the rules on age limits—over 65 years for a veteran and under 19 years for a junior—are particular to both disciplines, as are the cartridge rules (loads of up to 36g (1¼oz) shot size no 6 to 9 being permitted). A wide variety of guns can be used for this discipline; major competitions are still won with high quality English side-by-side guns. Still in regular use are guns by Purdey, Holland, Boss, Greener, Stephen Grant, Laing, Boswell and, of course, Churchill. Amongst the high-quality foreign sidelocks, Fabri and Renato Gamba are very popular. The humble selfloader is also a good fast pointer for this sport; however, it is more normal to see either a Perazzi or Beretta pigeon-type gun winning the major events. As to chokings, this is of course dependent on the speed of the individual, but as the first shot will be taken at a minimum of 26m and up to a maximum of 46m for the second shot, you can see that the classic pigeon-gun borings of ½ choke followed by a full choke are usually correct.

I have presented but a very brief description of the exciting FITASC discipline of *Electrocibles*. It is one of those shooting sports which, like boxed pigeon, must be tried to be appreciated—you will either love it or hate it. Me? I've been hooked for years!

Pat Lynch is the ZZ Great Britain Team Manager.

PART 3
FURTHER ADVICE

7

Young Shots

Sam Grice

In the acquisition of any skill, we are told that 'practice makes perfect'—which, of course, it doesn't: only *perfect* practice makes perfect—*bad* practice makes even worse, since the repetition of faults simply ingrains errors in technique, style and mental attitude. Thus with bad practice, one can become brilliantly awful! When learning to shoot it is therefore imperative to establish a sound basic technique as the platform on which further success is built and developed along structured lines, whether for game shooting or competitive clayshooting—or indeed, for any sport you care to name!

All shots are obsessed with smashing the target or bringing down game birds. As a coach, I am obsessed with how it is done—the method of hand/eye co-ordination which moves the gun to put the shot smack on the target. So many fathers these days reflect wryly that, had they been taught properly when young, they would be better shots today, and often observe with some astonishment and no little pride the ability, confidence and success of their offspring. Of course a good coach is on to a winner with any young person who is keen to shoot. He is dealing with material relatively free from any faults, someone excited, motivated, eager to learn and succeed. With first-class coaching, all these elements can be channelled into success and self-confidence, built on safe gun-handling and a sound technique. With encouragement and 'perfect practice' this will produce at the least a safe, confident and accomplished shot, and at the most, a brilliant one.

So where does one start? Well, obviously with the youngster, boy or girl—yes, I have coached many first-class shots of the fairer sex and some are quite devastating at clays and game! Physical size and strength are the important factors, as the pupil must be capable of handling a gun safely. Young people are more often as mature, if not more so, than adults about gun safety and shooting. If taught properly, the two are bonded together as one in the pupil's mind and in his actions, and become integral parts of the pattern or sequence required to shoot successfully.

How does one go about finding a good coach? The CPSA will provide, on request, a list of qualified coaches in your area. Shooting magazines contain adverts for shooting schools. Courses for young shots are on offer at various times from the BASC and from reputable shooting grounds, or you can always locate the nearest clayshooting club, several of which have a qualified coach. But do make every effort to seek out a good professional coach, one who has the qualifications to teach, or through long experience has a high reputation, or both. He should have the skills, personality and enthusiasm to motivate a pupil with patience, humour and understanding, plus the ability to teach within that framework of discipline which makes each lesson enjoyable and constructive.

The cost of lessons may appear to be expensive, but nothing of real value comes cheap. They are an investment in a skill for life that will give enduring pleasure and satisfaction, more often than not at a fraction of the price of an expensive present that in time may well be discarded! For a small or young pupil, a half-hour lesson is quite enough to start with; it is often a good idea to share an hour's lesson with a friend if that can be arranged. Remember that even adults can become tired towards the end of an hour's intense concentration, so a lesson should not overtire young muscles and culminate in deterioration through fatigue and ebbing concentration. A lesson should always end on a successful note and a real sense of achievement.

And what of parents? Every coach's nightmare would be the no-nonsense father dragging along a nervous little boy who has had a go but 'refuses to swing through his targets'. Father then produces the family 'boy's' gun, a single barrel .410 with which great grandfather (a shooting legend) slaughtered vast quantities of wildlife. The gun's stock has obviously been made out of wood from the true cross and the gun itself been in the family since biblical time; it is, indeed, a venerable relic—but in spite of this, refuses to hit anything for its current user. The fact that the intimidated boy shoots from the right shoulder with a left master eye and often with both eyes shut tight (in terror), is apparently irrelevant—Great grandfather always said (very loudly) to keep both eyes open and give 'em plenty of lead—about 20 feet or more! Yes, a caricature I know—but then, every caricature is an observation with exaggeration of human faults.

A little closer to the truth is the father who automatically assumes that as he's paying for the lesson, he should stand behind the coach and pick up a few tips, whilst fixing his gaze on both coach and pupil. His offspring then tries to serve two masters, seeking not only the coach's approval but that of his father as well. A parent hovering nearby can make things unfair for both coach and pupil and be a distraction for both, and I insist that father remains in the car or well away from proceedings during my lessons.

Next we must consider which gun to start with—though we must recognise that most guns are made for adults, using average measurements for stock length, comb height, triggers and guards and neck or hand. All these can cause problems for the small shooter.

Let us firstly dismiss the .410 as a suitable gun with which to start. Even for an experienced shot, it is difficult to use and inconsistent against flying targets, and tremendous control is needed to place its tiny pattern, generally badly composed, with any accuracy or effect. I would certainly recommend the 28-bore as a very real and highly effective little gun, as is the 20-bore using a light 13/16oz load. Recoil on both will be minimal, and a shoulder pad can be inserted under the shooter's jacket to reduce this even further. Basically, so long as the gun can be used comfortably and is light enough with the correct length stock, it can be judged suitable.

Gun stocks made for adults are generally too long for the average

Make sure the gun fits and is being held comfortably

youngster, and will bruise the shoulder or upper arm, even with the fore-end hand tromboned back. Such as these will be awkward to hold and difficult to mount. However, it is a simple and fairly inexpensive matter to have the stock shortened; the piece removed should be retained to put back at a later date when the pupil has grown enough.

Adults with small hands can suffer from bruising caused by knuckle contact with trigger guards. A youngster's hands are usually small too, and in reaching for the front trigger, the middle knuckle of the second finger presses against the rear of the guard, inflicting a very painful and eventually unbearable knock with every shot fired, resulting in bruising and swelling of the joint. Quite often tape and bits of rubber are wound round the back of the guard to alleviate the problems; to some extent they do, but they don't remove the cause itself. The simple answer is to shoot using the back trigger only, which is easily reached even with small hands and fingers and leaves a gap between the guard and the knuckle of the second finger.

Quite often the neck of hand can be too wide for a youngster to grip firmly, widening the grip and lengthening the distance to the trigger. Consequently they lose grip, and the lack of control caused by this can cause facial bruising. It is usually over-under shotguns having a wide pistol grip that can be problematic here.

Further consideration is that of facial size and dimensions. Children's faces are smaller than those of adults, hence the comb heights are generally too low for the pupil to see clearly over the breech and rib, resulting in a right-handed shot with right master eye shooting consistently left of the target, as only the left eye can actually see the target. A comb-raiser of the appropriate height will solve this problem immediately, enabling the pupil to see his target all the way from the pick-up point to the killing point.

There are, of course, youngsters who are big enough to use a 12-bore with light loads from the very onset, and if comfortable, should be encouraged to do so. Where a young pupil does not have access to a gun of his own, there is much to be said for using a semi-automatic 20- or 12-bore on the shooting ground. The fear of recoil is removed and confidence is enhanced by using a gun which throws an effective weight of shot and a consistently good pattern.

Remember that a light gun is more likely to give a lot of recoil unless matched to a light cartridge; in any case, particular care should be taken to purchase and use the lightest loads available for comfort and confidence. A light 20-bore shooting a 1oz load is likely to inflict more recoil than a 12–bore shooting a 7/8oz load, as the heavier gun will absorb much of the recoil into its weight. Not only that, but a heavier gun correctly related to the pupil's size and strength will swing more steadily and smoothly, and will produce more consistent results, enabling the shooter to repeat more exactly the sequence of actions required to hit the target, thus building up a pattern to his technique and increasing his confidence.

During the lesson, frequent rests or breathers are advisable to ensure that the pupil's strength lasts the duration of the lesson; when he becomes tired by too many shots, the movement of the muzzles very often runs on a parallel below the line of the target, or the swing forward fails to establish adequate lead on a crossing bird. Fatigue in any sport results in under-achievement and consequent frustration. Most youngsters will, if given the chance, shoot until their aims drop off, but there comes a point when further shooting is non-productive and demoralising; a good coach will sense this point in a lesson and quickly bring things to a successful conclusion. This only serves to reinforce my opening remarks about 'perfect practice'.

Safety is, of course, the most important part of learning to shoot. The facts on safety are taken in by the brain and, if taught properly, then lodge in the gut: thus a potentially dangerous movement with the gun should produce the same instinctive reaction as putting one's hand in the fire—a gut reaction to recoil away from it. Youngsters quickly assimilate such knowledge and reactions, especially if safety is taught as an integral part of the whole shooting sequence on the stand or peg. Sensible behaviour and safety off the stand should also be covered, through further instruction on shooting etiquette, social behaviour and courtesy.

Clothing is important from the point of view of safety as well as for comfort, and shooting wear has evolved, like other sportswear, to be most suitable for the job in hand. It should provide protection where necessary, and be designed with a view to ease of mounting and swinging the gun. No sane person would wear running spikes, driza-bone coat and a top hat to play soccer, so the young shot should be sensibly equipped to shoot safely. Ear muffs or plugs are the most important piece of equipment, and thankfully, most people are aware of the damage that shooting can cause to unprotected ears, especially at an early age. There are several effective makes on the market, and a set should be purchased before embarking on lessons. However, any reputable school or coach should provide these as part of the lesson.

Clothing can jeopardise safe shooting if, for example, the pupil wears a coat with a large flapping collar, a big wrap-around scarf or a baggy or overlarge sweater. Just as bad is a jacket with flap breast pockets, zips, studs or rivets other than below the waistline; and smooth nylon jackets or waist-coats will cause the gun butt to slide about in all directions. The ubiquitous Barbour is fine as an outer garment, and for clayshooting a skeet vest is essential. It has a large pocket for cartridges and a non-slip shoulder patch.

**Sam Grice is pictured helping a young pupil into a good 'ready position'
for calling the target**

It is a good idea to equip a young shot with a hat or peaked cap which will protect the head and eyes from broken clays, cut down the glare from the sun, and keep the rain out of the eyes. Spectacles should have impact-resistant lenses—eyes are irreplaceable and this type of lens is readily available from opticians.

As in every sport, comfortable footwear is important. Boots, wellies or strong shoes are recommended for winter wear or in the wet; trainers are fine when the weather is dry. And finally, gloves: these are essential in the winter to keep the hands warm and for grip, and in summer a light pair will avoid sweaty hands on the gun's woodwork and barrels. The trigger finger should be cut or folded back. Dangerous to use are big, hairy woollen gloves as they are totally insensitive on the triggers and become sodden with rain. Bulky or constrictive clothing should be avoided, as it makes for awkward gun-mounting and a gun which no longer fits.

And so after all this, on to the first lesson—and be sure that you arrive a little early so that it can start promptly. What should you expect for your money? After the initial introductions, a good coach will chat to the pupil about his hobbies and interests, about sport or school, in order to establish an immediate contact and rapport. Then he will discuss the gun, and give his introductory safety talk and demonstration on safe gun-handling, and finally will test for master eye and the approximate fitting of the gun. A few dry-runs first, pointing the empty gun at a stationary object or two, then out with his pupils onto the ground proper, to look at the target. If learning on a skeet range, this would be station 1 Low House; if not, a steady incomer passing to the left of the pupil's shoulder. Using his eye and forefinger, the pupil can become accustomed to, and practise, picking up the target first with his eye and then with his pointing finger to track the target in flight. This establishes the two crucial factors required to hit any moving object—line and speed.

Properly mounted, the empty gun can now be made to do the same as the pointing finger—pick up the target with the muzzles and track it by pointing directly at it during its flight. When successful repetition is achieved, it is time to experience the concept of lead: pulling ahead of the target, as the final part of the sequence. This can now be practised using a snap cap so that the trigger can be pulled when the correct pressure of lead is established. So before even firing a shot, the pupil already knows and is practising a simple technique to ensure success in the execution by following an easily understood three-part sequence.

Finally, with the coach taking full control of the gun and cartridges, the gun is loaded and placed correctly in the pupil's shoulder. The three-part sequence is followed: 'See it, point at it, pull ahead and fire', and the target is blown to dust, then gun down and open. And you have on your hands a youngster often astonished, thrilled beyond words and itching to do it again. All this is based on perfect practice, giving perfect results from the very start. After a few more successful shots and further praise and encouragement, plus reiteration of the sequence, the pupil can be moved round by a few yards to the right, and the whole business from finger-pointing onwards begun again, remembering that the lead required will now be bigger. The process and concepts are understood and further success follows—by which time the lesson should end with its aim and objectives achieved.

Once the basic technique has been executed successfully with the gun pre-mounted, then provided the pupil is physically capable, gun-mounting can be introduced. The pupil now has firmly in his mind the sequence of actions and the concept of lead required to hit the target. He can then concentrate on putting his movements in the right order, knowing that if the sequence is followed correctly, the target will break. It is amazing how quickly even young pupils can analyse an error in technique, and by going back to basics, put it right—back to perfect practice making perfect results.

Sam Grice is a schoolmaster, a CPSA senior sporting and skeet coach, and the proprietor of Long Acres Shooting School at Great Wilbraham, near Cambridge. He is an outstanding coach who has taken the Leys School Team to unrivalled triumphs in the Independent Schools Championships.

A skilled teacher, his lessons are a pleasurable experience and he certainly gets excellent results from all his pupils, whether they are experienced or novice shots. He is perhaps unique in his experience and understanding of coaching juniors from eight to eighteen, and in the sheer numbers that he has taught. Founder and organiser of schools' competitive clayshooting, he is the driving force behind the establishment of clayshooting as a recognised sport in the independent sector.

8
Guns:
Purchase and Care

Desmond Mills

I have been connected with the gun trade for over forty years and can vouch that there has never been a better choice of guns available than there is today. Although little development has taken place in the conventional side-by-side model, vast amounts of money have been invested in the high-tech machines and more sophisticated design required to produce over-and-under guns that meet the very high standards demanded by competition clay pigeon shooters. The over-and-under has characteristics which have proved to be more advantageous on demanding clay targets; for example the extra weight is an aid to recoil, and at the same time reduces muzzle flip. The narrower sight plane is a strong argument in its favour. And because of the aforementioned large investment in sophisticated machinery, the world's major gun manufacturers offer high quality models which are built to last a lifetime, and yet represent outstanding value for money.

For the shooter who has recently taken up the sport, the question of buying the right gun can be a very daunting one. Basically there are three different types, the side-by-side, the over-and-under, and the automatic. The side-by-side model was developed for the purpose of shooting game and is seldom seen in the field of competition clay pigeon shooting. The over-and-under is without doubt the most popular and widely used model, with the automatic being the second.

You will have to ask yourself what type of gun is required for the type of shooting you wish to participate in. Is the gun to be used for both clay and game shooting? If so, which will the gun be used for most? Perhaps you want to shoot clays, in which case which discipline? Perhaps you will want to shoot more than one discipline? The other very important factor is your budget.

All these questions need analysing very carefully, but once you have done so, it will make the purchase of your gun and model that much simpler.

Buying and Owning a Gun

The vast majority of guns, be they new or secondhand, are sold through three different outlets: gun shops, auction rooms and privately owned. Like any other business, shops rely on profit for their existence. The most successful gun shops provide a before-sales advisory service from staff with a certain level of expertise, plus an after-sales service to their customers. There are many excellent gun shops in this country, but there are also those which offer little in the way of expertise, or after-sales service. Their prime aim is simply to sell guns, and they give little thought as to whether the gun is actually suitable for the individual or his requirements.

It is always worth asking other shooters which establishment they use and would recommend, though you may have to be prepared to travel some distance in order to acquire the best service and advice, rather than just paying a visit to the local gunshop. All too often the first-time buyer assumes that the person standing behind the counter of a gun shop is an expert, an assumption that can prove costly. Thus you should never be in a hurry to purchase your first gun, but rather take your time in seeking advice, and read as much literature on guns as possible. Consider taking along a friend who has some experience of shooting and guns; his advice may well be of considerable help and could possibly prevent you from buying the wrong gun—though remember, at the end of the day the final decision must be yours.

Your very first visit to a gun shop should be exploratory, and you should come away with the feeling that good, sound advice was given from the other side of the counter, from a sales person who quickly developed an understanding for your requirements, expectations and needs. At no time should you feel in any way pressurised, or that the sales person was concerned only to make a sale.

Buying a new gun

One advantage of purchasing a new gun is that it will not be suspect with regard to the law appertaining to proof, since all new guns sold must be submitted to proof-house tests before being offered to the public. There are two proof houses in this country, in London and Birmingham, and many foreign makers have their guns sent to one of them; the relevant markings will be seen clearly stamped on both barrels and action. Guns manufactured in Italy and Spain have their own proof houses and are stamped accordingly, as these meet the very strict rules and tests imposed by the guardians of British proof.

Once you have decided on the make and model that you wish to purchase you should carry out your own inspection of the gun before you part with your money; if possible, make arrangements with the shop to try the gun out on some clay targets, preferably with a shooting instructor and gun-fitter. Inspect the woodwork on the stock and fore-end to ensure there are no marks or cracks. Look down the barrels for quality of presentation— they should be highly polished and smooth. The blueing or black should be deep and even. Assemble the action and stock onto the barrels and check that the fore-end bits can be removed easily. Finally, try opening and closing the gun.

Most new guns will be stiff and tight, which, as the owner of the gun shop will no doubt explain to you, is quite normal as the gun will need to be shot in. After a few boxes of cartridges have been fired through the barrels the stiffness will disappear, and the operation of opening and closing will become smooth and crisp. Nevertheless it is always worth carrying out the checks suggested, as sometimes damage does occur to guns in transit from importers to gun shops.

If you purchase a new gun you do also have the advantage of a guarantee; should anything go wrong, the gun can always be returned.

Buying a secondhand gun from a gun shop

First, set yourself a limit on the amount of money you wish to spend. Second, it is always a good idea to list the features you are looking for regarding barrel length, choke borings, whether you want full or semi-pistol grip, stock, make and model of gun, fixed choke or multichoke. Visit one or two gun shops which you know offer a full and varied range of models so that you can compare price and quality. Don't forget to inquire if the shop provides a repair service should anything go wrong with the gun, and whether a guarantee period is offered with the secondhand sale. You should also consider the possibility that you may wish to sell the gun at a later date because you want to purchase a better and more expensive model. Therefore find out what sort of price it is likely to fetch, particularly with regard to its trade-in value against a new gun.

Once you have considered all of these very important factors, and before you return to the gun shop of your choice, draw up a comprehensive list as

Desmond Mills watches a skilled gunmaker at his workbench

to what you should check and look for before you part with your money. Because a gun looks good, it does not necessarily follow that it is safe and mechanically sound. So take your time to check what you are thinking of buying. Go through the gun in a logical sequence using your check-list, starting with the barrels, then the action and finally stock and fore–end.

Request that the bore size of both barrels is officially measured—specialist measuring equipment is required in order to check that the gun meets the rules of English proof. All guns intended for use with nitro-powder must bear solid proof marks at the time of sale, and they must be 'in proof'—that is, the barrels must not have been enlarged beyond a certain size after they have passed the proof test.

These rules are for the protection of the customer; proof marks stamped on a gun do not necessarily mean that the gun is 'in proof'. Make a note of the sizes taken, as this information will be required at a later date. Now ask for the barrel wall thickness to be measured, and jot the sizes down on your check-list. There is nothing specific laid down in law as to a required maximum or minimum barrel wall thickness, but there have in the past been imported guns which, although they were legally in proof on the internal bore diameter, when readings were taken of the barrel wall thickness they were shown to be a lot thicker one side of the tube than the other. Such guns should be avoided at all costs. If the vendor refuses when you request the bore sizes and barrel wall thickness measurements to be taken, then I would suggest you buy elsewhere.

Examine the internal bores for any sign of dents or bruises; such obstruction would constitute a safety hazard should the gun be used. The best way of checking the bores is to hold up the barrels to the light some eight to ten inches away from your nose. Keeping both eyes open, look carefully down the bore, using the light so it throws a cone of shadow the full length of the tub e. Gently turn the barrels round through a full 360°: check for general condition, pitting, corrosion or leading. Now position the barrels so as to examine them on the outside, viewing them in exactly the same way. Having satisfied yourself that all is well, inspect the ribs for any sign of lifting away from the tubes, small pin holes which would allow the ingress of water. If the barrels feature a ventilated rib, look for signs of the rib being dented.

Inspect the general condition of the blueing or black, whether it has started to wear off, and if the nose ends of the barrels are nicely rounded, or dented and burred. In the case of barrels that have screw-in chokes, use the choke key to remove these and check them for thread damage; also take a close look at the internal threads in the tubes. Finally, the barrel lumps and barrel face: barrel lumps should be smooth and highly polished, not marked with deep score-lines where small particles of dirt and grit have got between the lumps and slots of the action when the gun has been closed, and which indicate neglect in gun cleaning. Examine the bite (where the bolt locks the barrel to the action) for signs of wear. If the gun has a full-width cross-pin the hook on the barrels should be smooth, and free of burrs and bad marks. Check the face of the barrels to see if they are pitted, and finally the extractors for any sign of undue wear before placing the barrels on the counter.

The Action

Whilst most of the actual mechanism is hidden from the eye, examination of the exterior is well worth carrying out. The general appearance should be one of crispness and general well-being, and not one of tiredness and neglect. Starting with the action face, look for the tell-tale signs of pitting, especially around the striker holes. Are the ends of the strikers smooth, nicely rounded and free of flats and pitting? If not, they will need replacing. Check where the barrels fit onto the action for any signs of bad score-marks.

Now move down to the cross-pin, which may be the full width of the body: does it show undue signs of wear? Is it slightly oval in shape? In the case of guns that use half- or button cross-pins, examine them for wear and general disfigurement. One of the most important areas of the action is the knuckle, because the fore-end iron pivots on this and helps to achieve smooth opening and closing of the gun. Again, it should be highly polished and without deep score-marks. The trigger guard should be free of dents and burrs which would indicate that possibly the gun has been dropped or knocked. The quality of screw- or pin-heads is always a good indication as to whether or not the gun has been stripped down by an amateur or a qualified gunsmith.

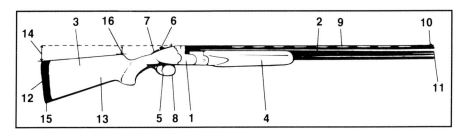

1 Action; 2 Barrel; 3 Stock: 4 Fore-end: 5 Trigger; 6 Top lever; 7 Safety; 8 Trigger guard;
9 Ventilated rib; 10 Front sight; 11 Muzzle; 12 Butt plate (or recoil pad); 13 Stock length;
14 Drop at heel; 15 Toe; 16 Comb height

Stock and Fore–end

The fit between metal and wood should reveal no gaps, and the wood should stand just proud of the metal. One of the weakest areas of the stock is the head, where the wood meets the back of the action, the top strap and the trigger plate: look for any signs of cracks or splits. Another weak point is the hand or grip, and you will have to examine this area very closely as the chequering can hide the tell-tale signs; in the case of side-lock guns, a very common place is immediately behind the end of the lock plate. Chequering should be crisp and clean cut, so take note if it has started to wear; there may be double lines which would indicate that somebody had tried to re-cut it at some stage, and not very successfully. Wood that features dark rich figure is a joy to behold and the envy of many, but do not let it mar your judgement when examining the stock which should be free of bruises, dents and deep scratches. Of course you must allow a certain amount of marking for fair wear and tear, but check both the toe and heel of the stock to ensure that they have not been badly chipped or bruised.

Finally, examine the fore-end wood and fore-end iron: starting with the wood, look to see if any small cracks or splits have started to appear where it meets the rear of the fore-end iron. This generally happens because the wood has to be cut away to accommodate part of the ejector work on many models. Check the kickers, the two metal protrusions to be found one on each side of the fore-end iron: are they worn or badly burred? Is the actual knuckle marked and scored, or the outer edge of the iron disfigured or burred? This is possibly because when the gun is opened to the full, the fore-end comes into contact with the underside of the action body.

Once you have completed both the check-list and a visual examination, you are in a better position to assess the overall condition of your intended purchase. However, before you make the final decision to accept or reject the gun in front of you, there are three practical tests that you should carry out that will give valuable information as to how safe the gun is, and its mechanical soundness. They are as follows:

1 Quality of fit between barrels and action
2 Effectiveness of ejector mechanism
3 Quality of trigger pulls

Such tests are not difficult in themselves, but in order to carry them out experience in the handling of guns is important, since they depend upon the individual's sense of feel and touch. Various mechanical movements are imposed on the gun so that, through certain working components selected elements of the mechanism are called upon to function. As a consequence they transmit their movement and hence quality of fit through the hands of the user, whose sensitivity of touch will identify what he feels.

The fit between action and barrels

The life of any gun is dependent upon the joint of the action to the barrels. It is possibly the most exacting operation that the gunmaker has to perform, for the safety and working life of the gun depends upon as near perfect a fit as possible of the barrels to the action. When a gun is loose due to wear between the two parts, this is often referred to as 'headache'. Correcting the fault can be a costly one, since the gun will have to be rejointed and the barrels brought back onto the face of the action. A simple yet effective test to reveal whether the gun is loose on the barrels can be conducted as follows: first remove the fore-end; carrying out the test with it attached to the gun will only produce a false picture, as the fore-end helps to push the action tight onto the face of the barrels.

With the fore-end removed, hold the gun with the barrels pointing upwards; now place the butt end of the stock on your groin with the right hand holding the grip or hand of the stock. Gently try to shake the gun up and down. If the gun is loose, you will feel movement of the barrels in the action. Now remove the gun from your groin, and place the stock close to your body and under the right arm whilst still holding the gun by the hand with the barrels pointing away from you and parallel with the floor. Stretch the fore-finger of the hand holding the stock along the right-hand side of the panel of wood known as the head of the stock, with the left hand gripping the barrels just in front of the barrel loop. Try and move the barrels from side to side. It is possible that you will experience some slight movement in a gun that has a high profile action—in layman's terms the action has 'high side walls'—but on no account should it be excessive. A gun that is loose at the joint will never, ever get better, but will get worse and should be rectified by a practical gunsmith.

Checking the ejector mechanism

Never be impressed by the vendor who, when demonstrating the efficiency of the ejector mechanism, sends the snap caps flying out of the gun to finish up halfway across the shop floor. The secret is to let the various parts of the mechanism work for themselves, which is achieved by opening the gun as slowly as possible. Having placed snap caps into the gun, pull the trigger. Many over-and-unders work on recoil for the second barrel, so a sharp tap on the butt end of the stock with the heel of the right hand will allow the trigger to be pulled for the second barrel. Hold the gun in the left hand, with your hand placed under the knuckle of the fore-end and base of the

In the Beretta factory, Desmond has a gun fitted

action. Push the top lever fully open with the thumb of the right hand, whilst at the same time gripping the small of the stock. Allow the gun to open but just a fraction. Now remove the right hand completely. Push the gun away from your body with the left hand, and now very gently tap the heel of the stock with your right hand, at the same time taking care to listen to the mechanism. You will hear a little click which indicates primary ejection has taken place; continue tapping the heel of the stock until the gun is fully open. The snap caps will do one of several things:

1 Eject together, clear of the gun, in which case the ejector mechanism has been regulated and timed so that it functions correctly
2 Not eject at all
3 One snap cap ejects whilst the other remains within the chamber, in which case something could be broken
4 Both snap caps fail to eject from the gun but hit the face of the action, indicating that the timing wants regulating
5 One side ejects whilst the other hits the action facer. Ejecting too early also needs regulating

The more slowly you open the gun, the better the picture you will have as to how effectively the ejector work is functioning.

Opening the gun very quickly and pulling the barrels downwards with the left hand in effect only helps to throw the snap caps out of the gun and assists the working of the mechanism. I would add that the use of snap caps is no more than an aid to check the function of the ejector work, and a true picture can only be achieved by the use of live cartridges. It is not unknown to carry out the test in the workshop where everything works perfectly, yet on taking the gun out onto a shooting ground with live cartridges it failed to operate correctly. This could be due to a fault in the mechanism which could almost certainly be attributed to wear or even the barrel chamber being oversized.

Using live cartridges and testing the gun under normal conditions would also highlight the problem of the extractors riding over the rim of the cartridge case. I would add that this is not a common occurrence but nevertheless it does happen.

Trigger pull

The final test to be carried out is that of the trigger pull. Trigger pulls are normally checked for poundage—that is to say, the weight is measured on a spring balance that is applied to the trigger in order to lift the sear out of the bent of the hammer in order to let the tumbler move forward onto the striker. The usual poundage set on the majority of guns is 3½ and 4½. Whilst you may not have a trigger pull balance, much information can be gained by the sense of feel and touch. With your snap caps in place and the gun closed, concentrate entirely on the trigger finger that is about to pull the trigger. Don't snatch at the trigger, but pull it as gently and as slowly as you can, at the same time giving your full concentration to the feel in your trigger finger and the movement of the sear out of the bent that is cut in the hammer. Your experience will be one of the following:

1 Sharp, crisp pull set to a suitable poundage
2 Very light pull, hardly touched the trigger
3 Finger on the trigger a long time to lift the sear out of the bent, in which case you are feeling drag
4 Trigger takes a lot of pulling to release sear, result heavy trigger-pull poundage.

Very light trigger pulls can result in the gun being dangerous to use, for obvious reasons. Alternatively heavy trigger pulls are just as dangerous, and should be rectified by a competent gunsmith before further use. The test of checking the quality of the trigger pulls will need to be carried out two or three times before a decision is made as to their quality, safety and suitability to the individual.

The time has now come to assess your overall findings and refer to your check-list. It may well be that all your checks proved positive and nothing untoward was found, in which case your decision is that much easier. Many gun shops check over guns purchased from clients before these are offered for re-sale, and any repairs needed are carried out. This may be brought to your attention by the vendor, on your request to inspect a particular gun that he has on his rack. Nevertheless I would always insist on carrying out your own examination to satisfy yourself that you are purchasing a gun that is 'safe' and in good overall condition. If you find something that is not to your liking during your examination, then bring it to the attention of the vendor and inquire if he will carry out the work prior to purchase. Having made the decision to purchase, ask for a bill of sale: this should include the bore measurements of both barrels, together with the barrel wall thickness, also the guarantee period. On no account should this information be accepted only verbally. If the gun shop is not prepared to submit your request on headed notepaper, then my advice is to leave well alone and try elsewhere.

Should an automatic be under consideration, then request the vendor to strip it down. You will note that it contains very few parts, and careful examination should reveal any undue wear or tear. Check the quality of the receiver, woodwork, blueing and general condition of the barrel, and don't forget to have the internal bore measured.

Many secondhand guns are purchased through advertisements placed in shooting magazines, local newspapers, the notice board of your local clay pigeon club or through mutual friends. If you are contemplating the purchase of a gun through any one of these outlets then I would strongly advise that you approach the transaction with caution.

Insist that the gun is examined by a practical gunsmith, and that you receive a detailed written report concerning the gun's bore size and wall thickness; this report should also state the gun's general condition, highlighting aspects that may need some fine adjustment or repair. If at all possible try and arrange to shoot the gun at a shooting ground on a variety of clay targets. Normally a small fee will be charged for examining the gun, and this should be paid for by the gun's owner.

I would remind any gun owner who is contemplating the sale of a gun that it is a crime under the Gun Barrel Proof Act to sell, or offer for sale, a gun that is out of proof. Heavy penalties will be imposed on those who flout the act. Ignorance of the law relating to the sale of unproofed weapons is no excuse. Having decided to purchase the gun, then the relevant police authority must be informed, with the information sent by recorded delivery and the relevant details entered on your shotgun certificate.

Secondhand values

As with many personal possessions, when the decision is made to either exchange them or realise their value in terms of money, one is very often surprised at the figure offered. If we take the period from 1980 to the present time, guns of reputable make have realised some very high prices on the secondhand market, with the record price being paid for a matched pair of game guns in the mid-eighties. In more recent years the price has somewhat declined, and the sale of secondhand guns greatly reduced. As a general rule there is no fixed secondhand price for your particular gun. At the time you decide to sell it is a question of obtaining the best possible price on the day: there is no *Glasier's Guide* on secondhand guns available to the gun trade. The assessment of a gun's value is made on an individual basis, backed by experience and current market trends and values, and of course makes and models.

When making the decision to purchase a gun, you will undoubtedly have a sum of money that you are prepared to spend. At the same time you must also be prepared to lose a percentage of the initial price should you decide to sell at some later date. We have all heard of cases where guns have been sold and have realised much more than their original pur-chase price, but such cases are in the minority. Nevertheless, as a gun owner you can do a great deal towards helping to maintain the true value of your gun—quite a part from which you have a moral obligation to ensure that it is kept in a safe and serviceable condition. It is always a good idea to have your gun checked over at least once every two years by a practical gunsmith, who will strip it down and examine the various components for any signs of wear or malfunction before giving them a thorough cleaning, then re-assembling. The cost for such work is minimal since it may prevent a malfunction in the shooting field which could spoil your day's shooting.

Cleaning and Maintaining your Gun

It is a well-known fact that a well-cared-for gun is one that will last longer, be more reliable, and will fetch a high price should it be traded in. All that is required is a few minutes spent on ensuring that your gun is put away clean after it has been used. Never be tempted to forego cleaning your gun after use, or leaving it overnight in a gun slip or gun case. Guns sweat badly, and moisture turns into rust which will eat into the surface of your barrels. An essential part of your cleaning equipment is a rod, together with woolmop, phosphor bronze brush, barrel-cleaning patches, clean cloth and either a feather or a pipe cleaner.

Using a clean barrel patch on the end of your rod, push it through the barrels to remove any dirt or fouling. Using several clean patches, repeat the operation until on withdrawing the patch it remains clean. Wipe both the nose ends and the face of the barrels with your clean cloth, and also the barrel lumps and under the extractors. Barrels that feature ventilated top ribs need particular attention to ensure that they are cleaned properly, as this can be a real moisture trap which will promote rust. A piece of cloth wrapped around a small knife blade will allow you to go between the rib vents.

Finally, always wipe the outside of the barrels over with a little oil applied to your cloth. Before putting the barrels away, the final operation is to apply a thin film of oil on the lumps and bites. If your barrels are fitted with screw-in chokes these should be removed and cleaned of the spent powder and residue which find their way into the threads in the barrel. A small bristle toothbrush is ideal for both the internal threads and those on the actual choke. Before inserting the choke after cleaning, apply a thin film of oil or grease to the thread and ensure that the choke is correctly seated using the special choke key.

The action body needs to be wiped clean, with particular attention being paid to the face, knuckle and flats. Actions which have slots to accommodate the barrel lumps require thorough cleaning to prevent scoring; at no time should you use an aerosol can to spray oil into the striker holes. Having ensured the action is clean, now apply a thin film of oil or grease to the knuckle. Finally, wipe over the exterior surface of the action with a clean cloth that contains a small amount of oil, to include the top lever, strap and trigger guard.

Stock and fore-end

The woodwork should be kept dry; simply wipe it over with a soft clean cloth. If your stock has been treated to an oil finish, then once or twice a year apply a light coat of conditioning oil. This should be palmed into the wood until no oil is left on the surface. A good rubbing using the palm of the hand will quickly restore your stock to its former glory. On no account allow the oil to penetrate the chequered areas of the stock or fore-end. If the chequering looks dull and dirty, give it a stiff brushing with a small nail-brush, but make sure this is the bristle type. The most common fault made when cleaning guns is to apply an excessive amount of lubricant, in the belief that it will give better protection. In fact, it will do more harm than good, as small particles of dirt and grit adhere to oil and grease, causing major problems when two working surfaces come together, apart from which oil will, in time, soak into the wood of your stock and cause it to rot. The gold rule to apply when cleaning is simply to wipe it on and then wipe it off, just leaving a thin film for protection.

**Gunmaker Gordon Swatton polishes a stock;
properly looked after, a gun will last a lifetime**

9
Tips from the Top

One aspect of clay pigeon shooting which has interested me over the years is that special breed, the champion shot. Not just the name who wins locally, or the crack shot who wins a couple of major titles, but the Nick Faldos or Nigel Mansells of the shooting world, those performers who have that little bit extra. One factor which they have in common is their utter dedication. Others come and go, but each discipline has a small group of individuals who consistently account for honours, and at every major championship theirs are the names which immediately go into the frame as competitors to be reckoned with.

By their level of consistency they command respect, and they invariably present a perfect role model for others, showing what can be achieved with application. I have selected four as representatives of the different disciplines; two are from the 'old school' and have been on the scene for some years, the other two are relatively 'new' boys who have made their mark on the sport in the last four or five years, sweeping all before them.

Talking to true champions is a fascinating experience, and I have always felt that much can be learned by discovering the way in which they got into the sport, what appealed to them, and how they progressed. Even if we do not share their ambitions for making it to the very top, there is much to be drawn from the way in which they have taken their talent to the highest of levels. And something which they have in common is their readiness to share their journey with others. The four who contribute here, for instance, while deadly serious when competing, are always prepared to help any beginner on the road to improvement. Indeed both Peter Boden and Joe Neville are outstanding coaches in their own right who have done a great deal to further the sport as a whole.

If we observe individuals such as these and consider them as role models, we can learn much about the ingredients for success. While dedication and self-improvement are key fundamentals, there are other more practical conclusions which inevitably they have drawn from their years at the top and which can be of benefit to others. If, for instance, someone with a string of national titles under his belt tells you that it is essential to avoid a certain type of gun or stance, then you have to acknowledge that what he is saying has good foundation!

The four clay shooting champions who have given us the benefit of interview here, are without exception fine ambassadors for our sport, and will remain true competitors and sportsmen for as long as they are able to hold a gun.

Stuart Clarke

Stuart Clarke was twenty-five before he took up clay pigeon shooting, but within five years he had made the Great Britain FITASC Sporting team, a rise to the top which must fall into the meteoric category. However, this is coloured by two factors—he was only eleven years old when he fired his first gun; and during his teenage years and early twenties, woodpigeons rather than the clay variety accounted for most of his spare time.

He shot clays once a year at the local Young Farmers' shoot near his home in Harlow, in Essex, but at heart he loved pigeon shooting. However, in time he found that so did an ever-growing number of other people, to the extent that it was becoming increasingly difficult to guarantee getting sport. 'There were so many people taking up pigeon shooting, the pressure on woodies was becoming so great that I really wasn't getting much shooting. So I decided to have a go at clays.'

He went along to his local Colliers' End clay club and found that his pigeon-shooting skills stood him in good stead. He realised, however, that his AYA Yeoman side-by-side was not quite the right gun for the job, and eventually moved on to a Browning B2G. 'The old Yeoman was choked half and full, which is probably why I still can't shoot a gun with anything less than half choke!' In his first year with the club he represented them at the Winchester Clubman Final. He joined the CPSA, attended his first registered shoot (at Fisher Reeves) and got himself into B class. The 27½in Browning gave way to a 30in and Stuart was in business. He got a draw in B class when shooting the British Open in 1985, and that same year competed in his first FITASC sporting competition.

'Andy Anderson (a friend at the local club) said I shot quite quickly with the short Browning and that I ought to give FITASC a try. I wasn't too sure what to expect, but that first competition made a big impression and I took a distinct liking to it. It is the sheer variety of FITASC with so many different ent targets which makes it so special. Of course by now I had seen all the big names of the time—Gerry Cowler, A.J. Smith, Barry Simpson—and I knew that's where I wanted to be.

'It was in fact Barry whom I saw on that first registered shoot who probably inspired me to greater heights. I remember seeing him straight a stand, absolutely drilling each and every target. I too managed a 10, but bits and chips everywhere. I wanted to be able to shoot like Barry had done.

'It was also Barry who persuaded me to change my gun, resulting in my purchase of a Beretta 682 Super Sport in 1988. This was the year when it all started to happen, as I won the British All Round, and I shot for England for the first time. I also won bronze in the Beretta World Sporting, the first of four successive bronze medals until winning the event in 1992.'

The following year he finally made the Great Britain team, though not without first losing a shoot-off for a place in the European (to Duane Morley); however, he then earned his place outright in the World

Championships in Villars, Switzerland. At the time of writing Stuart has been a team member ever since, winning no fewer than six team gold medals, two individual bronze and one individual silver. He won the British title in 1990, World Cup in 1991, then in 1992 completed a grand slam of British and English Grand Prix and UK Championships, along the way winning three successive GB team selection shoots; plus another bronze medal in the European Sporting Championship. Inevitably he topped the FITASC sporting team selection averages, and also the English sporting team selection rankings, with a top five placing in all five selection shoots, two of which he won outright.

This is a staggering record of both success and consistency. Consistency is what Stuart strove for in the first place, and it is that which ultimately brought him the glittering prizes. 'Like everyone, my aim was to improve, but as I got better I realised that the only way to compete at the top level was to become consistent.'

Waiting his turn and measuring the line of the target

So what has been his secret? 'Quite simply, hard work—don't get me wrong, I love my shooting and have a tremendous appetite for it, but the only way to make any real progress is by working at it. I have never shot an excessive amount, and I would say by far the most of the shooting has been in competition. But in the early days I practised every Wednesday at Chris White's Essex shooting ground where initially my aim was to shoot 25 straight at skeet. Then my goal was 50 straight, 75, and ultimately 100, which I eventually achieved in 1988.'

He feels that these were important milestones, both in terms of improved performance and also for learning the value of concentration. 'That is how skeet can be so good for you—it develops the kind of concentration which helps win shoots. You can never take any target for granted.'

His gun now is a Miroku 3800 32in. 'I went on to Miroku in 1990. Out of curiosity I tried a 32in then but it didn't seem right and I stayed with the 30in. I remember at the time I shot a 48 ex 50 with it, but found it such hard work, maybe because it was so different. Now, however, I use a 32in for everything, and I can shoot just as quickly with it.'

'Shorter 28in guns are much easier to handle, but in many ways too easy and there's a tendency to shoot too quickly. As mentioned earlier I also prefer tight chokes—I think that perhaps they force the shooter to be more careful and more accurate. With an open choke there's a tendency to think "that will do". Also with tight chokes you can see exactly where you are on a clay. Another little luxury they offer is that with a bad mount there is time to adjust the mount and get it right before taking the shot.'

'Not that I would recommend that this combination is ideal for anyone taking up the sport. Definitely opt for 28in or 30in, and more open chokes, until you find your own style. You can then change to something longer if you wish.'

Stuart is also a great believer in the importance of gun-fit. 'I have always been fussy about gun-fit—I feel it is very important. If the gun isn't quite right when you mount it, then the distraction can result in a miss. If you see anything of the side of a barrel when you are about to shoot, then there is a very good chance that you will miss the target.'

'This is something which my father has always instilled into me, and can only be gauged when you are actually shooting—it is possible to make virtually any gun fit when in a room, but when in action it's a totally different ball game. My own stock still isn't quite right, but I will work on it during the winter!'

Goodness knows what he will score when he gets it how he wants it!

For ammunition, Stuart uses 7½ on everything (RC cartridges, in this instance) and advises any shooter to use the best he can afford. 'George [Digweed] and Barry both use different shot sizes for different targets, but I tend to get distracted and I like to keep as many decisions as possible out of my shooting. My own feeling is that if a target is close enough to warrant a skeet shell, then the pattern wouldn't have a chance to spread out enough to benefit from the extra pellets.'

So what was the hardest part to master on the road to success? A difficult target perhaps? 'Not at all—in my own instance the toughest part of it, without question, was learning to handle the pressure. It's one thing getting into a good position, but it's another altogether to turn it into a winning score, or a potential winning score. There are thousands who can shoot really well, but my feeling is that it is how they handle the pressure which ultimately makes the difference.' So how had he come to terms with the problem?

A pause for concentration before calling a target

Looking and mounting as the clay comes into view

Head down and the target is broken

'Obviously the number of competitions I have taken part in has helped, but the bigger the shoot the more you feel that you are on your own. If you bottle up pressure it inevitably starts to affect your shooting. I try to develop a rhythm.

'It is best to empty the mind and almost let the shooting happen. If you think too much about any aspect of your shooting, then it can become too mechanical. You get stiff, stop your swing, and lose that all-important rhythm.

'To be honest, when I am shooting really well I don't even think about lead. If someone asked me after I have shot a target, how much lead I gave it, I wouldn't have any idea. Yet it might have been as much as eight feet. My own method of shooting has just evolved. I knew I had to pick a target up with the barrels, track and shoot in front. With a lot of pigeon shooting and then clays, my style developed from that basic fundamental to the point now where basically I look at the clay and shoot. Really I suppose it comes down to concentration on the clay to the exclusion of all else. Ultimately I have now come to rely on that technique—and also on experience to tell me instinctively how to shoot a target—it's a question of getting into the right frame of mind, so that in a way you almost let the shooting happen. It's a very finely tuned balancing act of being relaxed, yet applying concentration and aggression.

'I think it also very much depends on the way you are made. By nature I tend to be laid back, but obviously this isn't any good for winning competitions. Therefore I need motivation, but not to the extent that I become wound up with wanting to win. The desire to win has to be there, but not so strong that it gets in the way. Like everything else, it is something you have to work at.'

Clearly, for Stuart Clarke that work has rewarded him with substantial dividends.

George Digweed

There is one man above all others who is always the hot favourite, whatever the shoot he enters; such is the reputation of George Digweed. Since taking the CPSA's Jubilee Sporting Championship in 1988 he just hasn't stopped winning. Now twenty-eight, George is World and European Champion and has also shot record scores when winning the British Open sporting and skeet titles. His track record is formidable—but he hasn't always been a great shot: 'The first time I ever shot skeet at Catsfield, Sussex I scored 69 x 100.'

We must go back to George's childhood to pick up his first interest in guns and shooting. 'My grandfather always shot a lot of DTL and sporting, and used to do quite a bit of rough shooting. I would go with him and carry an old .410 over my arm—though he never let me have any cartridges! It was just so that I could get used to a gun.' Grandfather owned the butcher's shop in Hastings which George now runs. Eventually, of course, George took up the sport and as a thirteen-year-old he entered and won his first clayshoot, winning the junior trophy at the East Sussex WFA Open at Crowham Manor.

George Digweed –
eyes looking
back towards the
source of the target

His first gun was somewhat unorthodox: a 20-bore Winchester pump action with a Coutts compensator. 'It was my mother's old rook gun' he explains. Well, it certainly got this rookie off to a good start for George used it for two years until his grandfather handed him a Miroku 800HSW 26in over-under. However, he didn't get on very well with it, and went back to the pump gun before moving to a Remington 1100; this he used for the following three years, and really started making a name for himself.

In his first English Open DTL Championship and Dougall Memorial he shot 199 x 200. 'I shot 100/291 and 99/292 and never won anything!' He was seventeen at the time. He did win one major trophy as a junior, however, taking the British Double Rise under-18 title. Also in his last year as a junior he entered his first English Open Sporting Championship. 'It was the last year that it was held at Somerleyton, and Jeremy (Welham) was the winner. I finished fifth in the juniors. It was a good result for me—it gave me an idea of what I was up against and provided an incentive.'

From that point he stopped shooting trap and moved to sporting in an altogether bigger way. His nearest sporting ground was Catsfield which used to have some useful shoots, and George first won the county sporting

171

Sheer concentration as the gun is mounted

title there in 1983, at only nineteen. He has won it every year since, with the exception of 1990 when it clashed with the Dutch FITASC Grand Prix (which he won instead!). However, from winning at Catsfield he shot little else but skeet for the next two or three years. He knew he could shoot it, but it frustrated him, and this period gave a hint of what was to follow.

Frustration for George Digweed is invariably transformed into determination: 'I felt I was lacking concentration—I could shoot skeet but was never any good. I would get a score of 83–90 in the 100 bird shoots, hitting 22s, 23s and 21s. I became resolved to master it.'

Then one afternoon at a Catsfield practice shoot, his grandfather took along a Winchester 101 multi-choke. 'I shot 49 with it—my first 25 straight. I then went out the following Sunday and shot 94, and my scores started creeping up. Grandfather then took an old Miroku sporter out of the cupboard choked full and full, which I used for a Catsfield 100 registered skeet, and shooting on the last squad of the Sunday afternoon I bagged my first 100 straight.'

From then on there was no looking back, and at one stage he had an average of 99.2 over 1,800 targets. In 1986 he represented England for the first time in the Skeet Home International at Melton Mowbray, and shot 200 straight. His marathon record-breaking 475 straight for the British title was still to come, but George decided to quit competitive skeet at this point. 'I'm not exactly sure why. I had made the England team, and had shot 200 straight. I also recognised that no matter how good one got at skeet, there was always an element of luck in winning a major championship—it all hangs on one target. So from that point I decided to try and make the England sporting team.'

By now, he was using Parker Hale 800 trap and game guns: within one year he was in the England sporting team for the trip to Scotland. No big wins in 1987, but progress was good and his resolve strengthened. 1988 brought club wins, some good performances and an England sporting team place again; and then at the end of the year he won the CPSA Sporting Jubilee at Hodnet. When afterwards he told me that this was just the beginning, there was a temptation to think 'here we go again'—thoughts of future disappointments are rare indeed amidst the heady atmosphere of success. But somehow with George you knew that he meant it:

'The reason I said that was because having won a major title it gave me confidence. I knew I could do it.'

It was like shooting his first 100 at skeet, and the reality of what followed exceeded all expectations: never in recent history has the sport been so dominated by one man as it was by George Digweed in 1989. He tried yet more changes of gun. At Hodnet he had used a Browning AIT Sporter and Parker Hale trap gun, but during the winter he took up the offer of Beretta sponsorship and changed to a pair of 682s, trap and sporting, both 30in. There was simply no-one to live with him. He won the Saab–Gunmark at Mid-Norfolk, the English Open Sporting at Blandford, the British Open Sporting at Mid-Norfolk and the ICI Grand Prix at Doveridge: he literally swept all before him.

Gun firmly mounted, picking out a target

The following year he picked up from where he had left off, setting a course record of 97 in the Saab–Gunmark Super Sporting at Mid-Norfolk with some truly phenomenal shooting. And he was runner-up in the British Open Sporting Championship after losing a shoot-off to Gary Phillips; both had shot 96. In 1990 he also made his debut at FITASC sporting, and those who had thought the newly crowned king of English sporting would come seriously unstuck with the gun-down stipulation of FITASC once again underestimated the man. He won a string of four overseas Grand Prix events—the Dutch, Belgian, Swiss and EEC. He then returned home to win the UK Championship at the first attempt.

In 1991 he reclaimed the British Open Sporting crown with an outstanding performance at High Lodge, where his 89 was a remarkable score on a difficult course. He then claimed a bronze medal in the World FITASC Championships in Switzerland, and returned home to shoot his only skeet event of the year, the British Open at Kingsferry, Kent, winning with a staggering 475 straight. Anyone who saw him shoot on that August afternoon in Kent will have exactly appreciated the reasons for his continuing success: his concentration and his *will* to break each and every target, qualities which together make him absolutely phenomenal. There is no such thing as an easy target to George Digweed—every shot is a very serious business. He completed a remarkable 1991 by winning the American Sporting Championship in San Antionio, Texas, as well.

In the New Year of 1992, he made his mark early by winning the CPSA centenary shoot at Hereford, though interestingly it was to prove a year in which he particularly excelled on the international stage.

He entered three FITASC sporting shoots during the year (his work prevents him from entering non-championship two-day events) and won them all: the European at High Lodge with 177 in which he was four targets clear; then he completed the 'ultimate' double by becoming World Champion in Vermont, USA, where his 191 was not only six targets clear, it was also a world record score—the jealous critics who said it was an easy shoot conveniently overlooked his winning margin. Others reckoned it was just about the best piece of shooting they had seen. George admitted afterwards: 'It's the best I have ever shot—of the nine targets that I missed, I cannot think of one which in hindsight I should have hit.'

He followed this by taking the World Cup in Cyprus with 179, two targets clear of silver medallist Stuart Clarke. Despite this extraordinary hat-trick, the season was still not over; as a result of his win in the European, he collected a prize of a Browning gun, and was invited as a guest to the end-of-season Browning Masters both to participate (in the Guests' class) and to collect his prize. What followed was little short of sensational, because in competing over 250 targets and in eight different disciplines, George finished a staggering eleven targets clear with 227. As a guest he was obliged to use a Browning gun on one discipline—he chose skeet, and hit 25 straight. He had seen neither Double Trap nor Olympic Trap before, and shot 22 and 45 x 50 respectively. The 22 was the top Double Trap score of the day, vindicating George's indication that he will be looking to compete in this discipline at the 1996 Olympic Games in Atlanta, USA.

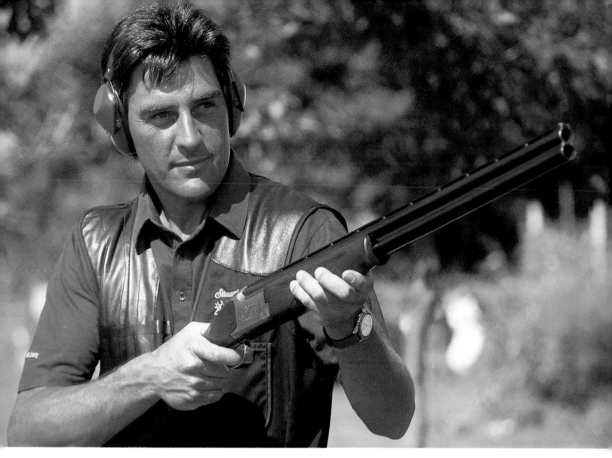

Stuart Clarke: a relaxed stance but ready to strike

Peter Boden with both eyes open as he picks out the target

Joe Neville shoots with both knees slightly bent; he is a great believer in absolute concentation on the target

Age is on his side (he will be thirty-two for the year of the next Olympics) and he even hints that the best is yet to come! So what has been his secret? Is it his stance, or was it the instruction he received as a teenager?

'I can't put my finger on it. Though my grandfather was very good to me as a teenager, I am totally self-taught.' The legs-astride stance came naturally to him (just as it had to A.J. Smith) and has been copied by thousands of clay shooters; his gun-hold is often short with the hand near the action. However, it has all been developed instinctively through trial and error.

'I think that one of the biggest contributory factors is that I am very competitive. I enjoy a lot of sports—cricket, tennis, golf, squash, fishing—and I am competitive in all of them, it is part of my make-up. However, I am not as good at any of those as I am at shooting—but then again, I have devoted an awful lot of time to shooting.' George will regularly visit three of more shoots on a non-championship Sunday. Prize-money is certainly a motivating factor, but is not the ultimate stimulus—it is winning and perfecting a talent that really spurs him on.

'It would be stupid to say that I don't go for the prize-money, because obviously it is always an attraction. But I think that practice can only improve your skills if it is in a competitive environment. Once you break the barrier of producing good scores under pressure, then you can believe in yourself and that's when the better scores start coming. Now I actually perform *better* under pressure.'

His will to win and his winning habit combine to make him a few enemies. He has a swagger and is not averse to winding up his critics—after winning the British Open Skeet Championship he even said that he wouldn't shoot skeet any more because it was too boring, and wrote a letter to *Pull!* to say that he was standing down to give some of the others a chance.

It was a bit of mischief which backfired on him—not everyone shares his sense of humour. There was a small minority who resented George's win, maintaining he was not a regular skeet shooter; presumably they had forgotten his 200 straight in the Home International five years earlier. But catch George in a serious moment when not shooting, and he will be the first to tell you that much of his success is based on the importance of concentration, and it was skeet which taught him this.

During the last four years he has also settled on a regular gun and cartridge combination, using the pair of Beretta 682s and Kent Champion ammunition (7s and 8s). He actually uses his trap gun, choked 3/4 and full, for a lot of English sporting, and interestingly he has not had the stock dropped: it is a high shooting gun, and the stock has a slightly unusual cast having been left in the warm one night after getting sodden wet whilst game shooting (is this perhaps his 'secret weapon'?!). As a consequence the two guns shoot very differently; both are 30in, but one is a flat-shooting sporter while the other is a high-shooting trap gun. Yet because he has shot so much with both, and with his uncanny ability to read targets, he can readily switch from one to the other; though he prefers to use the trap gun as much as possible, in line with a current trend among top sporting shooters towards tight chokings.

What about his style and sight picture? 'I honestly couldn't tell you.

George tracks a target in order to work out a method of attack for when he takes his turn

The method works! George is one step closer to winning the 1992 European Championship

Basically I come from behind and shoot on the swing, so it wouldn't be possible for me to tell anyone exactly how much forward allowance to give a certain target. It will all depend on the speed of the swing.'

George will never forget the year 1992, for it has also had a serious 'down' side. His father died during the morning of the final day of the World Cup in Cyprus; George missed the prize-giving to be at his bedside, but arrived home too late. It had been a protracted illness, and George very nearly didn't go to the World Championship because of it. 'In the end I realised that if I hadn't gone he would have realised that something was very seriously wrong. I am just fortunate that I had Kate (my girlfriend) with me through the year at the big shoots. We have been together for some time now and get on great, and I think that this has been an enormous help to me.

'On a trip to somewhere like America there can be so many distractions. But I went there in the hopes of winning, and because Kate was with me, was able to enjoy the trip without deviating from the objective of turning in a good performance.'

But then again, there is very little which would distract George from this objective. So this is a story which could run and run . . .

Peter Boden

For nearly twenty years Peter Boden has been one of Britain's finest trap shooters, although the last two or three have been very different to the previous twenty-two. From being a skilled precision toolmaker and an international trap shooter, he is now a full-time shooting instructor, and until recently a coach to the British Olympic trap team. Not that he has abandoned his shooting; in fact he has shot more scores of 190-plus since becoming a coach than at any time during a long and successful career.

It is a career which owes its origins to the many happy hours spent when he was young in Bedworth, where all his spare time was spent on a farm. Guns were a constant source of fascination, and at the age of eleven he got his first side-by-side. 'I pestered my father so much that he eventually relented and bought me a 12-bore.'

Now forty-three, Peter's views on first guns have altered little. 'My feeling is that if you are strong enough to hold and handle a 12, then this is the gun you should start with.'

Clay pigeons were far from his mind: it was all pigeons, pheasants, partridges. 'There was plenty of game in those days. Farming methods were different and there were many dairy farms and plenty of woodland. All you had to do was make a polite phone call. I had four or five farms to roam.'

He didn't have any taste of clays until he was sixteen. 'I thought it was a bit silly—you couldn't eat what you shot, so I didn't see much sense in it.' However, he went along with a couple of pals to a small local shoot armed with a box of Maximum 5s (1¼oz), and found that he could hit the artificial targets with relative ease.

His first proper shoot, however, was the Boxing Day competition at Berkswell. He entered for the DTL and Double Rise competition and won it.

Peter Boden – head well forward and everything focused on the target

'I only went because a couple of friends suggested it. My own gun—I had a Reilly by this time—had broken so I used a borrowed BSA.'

But it was another eighteen months before he started to shoot more seriously. 'Jack Wrighton, a local farmer whom I had known from a very early age, saw me shoot at an agricultural show and suggested that I should take it further. Following more prompting, he persuaded me to get my first over-under. It was a Browning A1 trap gun which I bought for £150, and I'll never forget—I bought the gun in the morning, and in the afternoon I won £10 with it!' He was eighteen at the time. Though he shot all the disciplines, he knew by then that he 'liked them going away'.

With the new gun he set about the nursery slopes of 25 and 50 bird trap competitions, with the occasional 100 for good measure. He still shot some sporting and went to a lot of different grounds. 'I think that's how I learned my shooting. I am self-taught and found I could benefit so much by watching a lot of people. I also feel that the overall experience of different disciplines and different grounds helped so much in developing my shooting.' His first big win came in 1969 when he became the British Double Rise champion at Doncaster. He won both the British and English titles the following year, and the English again in 1972.

While going-away targets were favourite, he shot well at DTL but didn't make significant headway. 'When it came to team selection I shot well for four or five hundred targets, but then lost interest. I just didn't find it as exciting as doubles.'

Almost inevitably he found himself on a trench layout. He shot the Welsh Grand Prix at Sealand: 'I shot 84 on the first day and was bitterly disappointed'. However, he found himself involved in other celebrations that evening, and suitably relaxed the next day, he finished with 50 straight for a 94 and second place. He had found his chosen discipline. After that his shooting was exclusively 15-trap and 5-trap, with the odd ABT for good measure. In that first year of competing in international disciplines he shot his way into the 5-trap team for his first overseas event. 'I had never travelled abroad before, so to shoot in Juan Le Pins was a little bit special!' Returning a score of 192 wasn't so bad either! Altogether it was an eventful year, for he also married his attractive wife Marilyn.

In 1973 he 'cracked the big time' and won the Olympic Trap British Grand. He also secured his first sponsorship deal, and from that year shot Gevelot cartridges.

Then followed a change of gun. 'I decided that I wanted something nicer and bought a Browning C3. Once again Jack was a great help.' But the results stopped coming. 'I had a mediocre year, but I think you mostly need time to adjust to a new gun. You may shoot well with it first time out, but if the fit isn't right and the feel is different, it will take time.'

In 1975 he got going. He won the British Grand Prix again, and qualified to shoot in both the European and World Championships. From then on there was no looking back. Olympic Games in Montreal and Los Angeles, British and English Grand Prix at Ball Trap, travelling the world as a regular team member, and although Britain didn't send a team for the Moscow Olympics in 1980, he compensated amply by winning the British, English and Welsh Grand Prix titles. He also collected Commonwealth Games gold and silver medals. Altogether it has been an ongoing story of success at the highest level.

There have been other gun changes along the way. In 1977 he changed to a Beretta SO4, switched to another SO4 in 1978, and finally an SO3 in 1980. By 1982 he had changed again, this time to a Parazzi MX8 SC3. 'Though I had shot well with the SO, which was a superb gun, and I was in the team which won a bronze medal in the 1981 World Championship, I just felt that I was ready for another change and challenge.' A change is as good as a rest! However, by now he knew precisely what he wanted in terms of gun-fit. Using the new Perazzi in 1982, he won the English ABT Grand Prix, was 2nd in the World Grand Mondial 5-trap and took Commonwealth Gold at Olympic trap in Brisbane. He had now also changed ammunition to Rottweil.

His own wins have never really stopped coming. But another landmark came in 1987 when he took junior shots James Garland and James Donoghue to the Polar Cup in Helsinki. This was a qualifying shoot for the World Cup. Peter shot a 194, but more significantly under his tutelage the two juniors performed superbly and the three together won the overall team gold medal.

Significantly, a chance conversation persuaded him to give up his tool-making job and become a full-time instructor at Garlands Shooting Ground. 'I only wish I had done it earlier.' The move to Garlands has worked well for everyone.

It was the added spice needed to revitalise his interest in the sport: by the end of 1987 he and Joe Neville had become official team coaches for the

British team, and since that time Britain has become a recognised force with results which at last match the promise.

There can be no doubting Peter's influence, although he is reluctant to take credit. 'We now have some very good shots in this country—what we lack are facilities. There are only six active Olympic trap grounds in the country, two of which are in Scotland and one in south-west Wales—that leaves only three grounds for the majority of population.' He was referring to North Wales Shooting School, East Yorkshire Gun Club and Garlands. There is no ground holding competitions south of Staffordshire. Small wonder that the Italians are amazed at the high standard of our shooters in view of such limited availability of practice and competition facilities.'

1989 saw great strides being made with Kevin Gill winning the World Cup, and the team taking gold in the Grand Prix of Europe. So why have we struggled for so long in international events? We return good scores but seldom *winning* scores.

'It's back to facilities. We also have weather conditions to consider in England—we are not used to returning the very high scores that win inter-national events. Consequently we don't have the belief in ourselves that we can actually get those 198 or 199s that win gold medals.

'But we have some very good talent now, so I expect that our international showing will continue to improve. You tend to find that winners put that bit more into it—they are more determined. Kevin Gill is a very good example—he has a lot of ability, but he is also very determined. He will get results.'

Peter's own style is a model of simple effectiveness. Clean and neat, he shoots with a minimum of fuss to a maximum of effect.

'I am a great believer in keeping it simple. A relaxed but positive stance should not involve any knee-bend or exaggerated movement. What is essential is a gun that fits—the dimensions must suit the man.

'I also like a good quality gun. Every gun that I have owned and used since the Browning C3 has been a high grade model with attractive engrav-ing and good wood. I feel that the makers will put more effort into a better grade gun so it is much more likely to be better overall. It must be worth spending a bit more on a gun which you can be proud to own—it will give its owner a touch more confidence.'

Olympic trap is a notoriously difficult discipline, so is it possible to coach people to shoot it with reasonable consistency? 'Definitely. You tend to find that many try it and then shy off because of some disappointing scores. But it's worth persevering with, and it is quite possible to get good scores. We recently had a gentleman called Karan Kamar visit us, on recommendation from India. He spent a fortnight with us and although he hadn't shot before, he shot a 25 straight on his very last round before flying home. It can be done!'

So what are the principal faults of the DTL shooter, as compared to the Olympic trap shooter? 'You see a lot of DTL targets shot too quickly, but rarely an Olympic trap target shot too slowly. Timing for both is so important. 'In both instances, far too many look at their gun when they shoot, measuring targets out. You should never take your eye off the target. Similarly if at all possible try to keep both eyes open—you don't drive a car with one eye closed. The lighter load is definitely not so tiring. You get no aching or after-effect from a two-hundred bird shoot. And of course they are steadier on second barrel shots.'

He talks with enthusiasm, but due to commitments was unable to continue as team coach. Having done a spell of two years, he felt that it was time to step down.

His coaching skills are, however, given full rein at Garlands where he copes readily with raw beginner and top competitor alike. 'It can be hard work but it's very rewarding. On company days we get a number of people who have never shot, and they are amazed to find themselves quickly becoming quite proficient. Plus it's all good for the sport as it continues to bring more and more people into the fold.'

His style is one that any beginner would do well to emulate. And so is his personality—it is always reassuring to discover that winners can also be nice guys.

Note the uncomplicated stance

Joe Neville

There are few brilliant shots who are naturally good coaches; an ability to teach is a skill all of its own. But one man who has definitely proved outstanding at both is Joe Neville. Arguably one of the greatest shots Britain has ever produced—certainly our finest skeet shot—Joe is now showing a considerable talent as a coach. His name may not be so familiar to the new generation of shooters whose attention is focused on the current stars of the sporting scene, since he retired from competitive shooting nine years ago; but he had an unrivalled record of success behind him. The fact that he was the first person in the world to shoot 200 straight under current ISU rules gives a fair indication of the calibre we are talking about.

He was born into a hill-farming family in the pretty Derbyshire village of Tansley, near Matlock. His father was not a shooting man, but his grandfather was gamekeeper for Lord Derby at Liverpool and also on the Waterhouses estate. Shooting was therefore in the blood, and Joe says: 'I was fascinated by shooting ever since I was big enough to hold a stick.'

He was actually twelve when he first pulled a trigger and took up rabbit shooting with a vengeance. 'All of my spare time was spent with dogs and ferrets—the cartridges were paid for by selling rabbits at half-a-crown a time!' He is still very keen on terriers to this day.

An introduction to clays came at a Young Farmers' shoot at Stanton-in-the-Peak when as fifteen year-olds he and a pal cycled with hammer-guns strapped to their bikes to take part. 'He was first with 4 x 5, and I was second with 3,' Joe laughed.

From the age of thirteen much time had been spent with the local pest officer Archie Hill. 'I have never seen anyone shoot game better than him. When we worked the dogs he stood upright holding a .410 pistol—his arm would swing smoothly like a pendulum and when a rabbit ran out he would knock it over in an instant. He was brilliant.'

Then Jess Bailey gave young Joe his first proper introduction to clays at Matlock Gun Club. Appetites sufficiently whetted, by the time he was eighteen, he and three or four pals were making a monthly visit to Clarrie Wilson's Little Mill Shooting Ground, near Rowarth, Stockport, where they would shoot 50 sporting. Under the guiding eye of Clarrie, his scores began to show a marked improvement. The turning-point came in December 1966: 'Clarrie asked me to consider the possibility of shooting ISU skeet, explaining that it offered the opportunity of representing Britain overseas, culminating in the Olympic Games. I took up ISU (Olympic) skeet that very day!'

Joe could see the possibilities. He had a goal and he was a very determined young man. 'I found it very difficult to start with, and learned what I could from people like Colin Sefton and Alec Bonnett. Obviously, Clarrie also helped.' In his first full year at ISU he shot 700 registered targets for an

Opposite
Joe Neville – an easy, legs apart stance

average of 79 per cent. The following year he improved, and shot 900 for 89 per cent and got into the British team for the international competition in Moscow in May 1969.

'I didn't get a very good score, but it was exciting to shoot with the Olympic champion and also the best lady shooter ever, Nuriah Otiz.'

He was twenty-five years old, and so began a spectacular career in which he represented Great Britain for eleven years. It was a career which came to an abrupt and unexpected end in 1980 with the Moscow Olympics—despite much political furore, all British sportsmen took part, *apart from* the shooting and equestrian teams! Thoroughly disillusioned, Joe called it a day.

His record was staggering. In all international competition he averaged 97 per cent. His first domestic double came in 1969 with the Welsh and British titles, then the following year he was second in the World Championship in Arizona. He went on to win the French Open, South African Open, Swiss Open, Spanish Open, the British title three times

Looking to the low house for the target to come into view

(runner-up seven) and the English six times. He was fourth in the Munich Olympics in 1972 with 194 (three shot 195).

His extraordinary 200 straight came in an Eley exhibition shoot at Holland & Holland. It could hardly have been better timed for the cartridge company, Joe having shot Gevelot until making the switch that year.

In competition he has shot four 199s, eight 198s and thirty-seven 100 straights.

After a five-year lay-off he was tempted back by the prospect of the Commonwealth Games in Scotland. He shot 199 in both of his first two qualifying shoots. In the Commonwealth Games itself he won a team gold medal, and a silver individual.

Now, Joe does only one or two competitions a year. Last year he shot the British Grand Prix at Blandford and took bronze. He also enjoys the odd FITASC sporting shoot and is a very keen pheasant shot, enjoying the privilege of belonging to a high-bird shoot in Derbyshire. 'I am a better game shot now that I no longer concentrate on skeet—to succeed in any discipline you have to concentrate exclusively on that and nothing else.'

But he again came close to great triumphs as coach to British teams, as he and Peter Boden proved a formidable duo in transforming the fortunes of the British teams in international competition. Our British trap and skeet teams had a long record of being 'nearly men' but 1989 changed all that, and under Joe and Peter's guidance they started to collect medals. The skeet team won the gold medal in the European Grand Prix of Nations, and Graham Taylor then took the individual gold in the European Championship in France.

Kevin Gill meanwhile won the Olympic Trap World Cup in Germany, and the team came back triumphant from the European Championship.

'We have a lot of talent coming through at trap, but we are struggling badly for skeet shooters. We have some terrific young shooters in this country but they don't seem to be attracted to Olympic skeet. In fact at present we have more class shooters than probably any country in the world. We could sweep the board.'

Unfortunately Joe can't see the situation changing. Olympic skeet is difficult and many are put off by disappointing scores; this also results in few grounds offering an ISU facility. In turn the discipline then becomes expensive and inconvenient because people have to travel to shoot it. But as Joe points out, with the incentive of taking part in the Olympic Games, one would have thought that more interest would be shown.

'There are one or two good youngsters such as Jason Mell, Andrew Melton and the Faulkner brothers—coach Jack Pennington did a good job—but generally there are few people promoting Olympic skeet, and even fewer coming into the sport.'

Joe's introduction to coaching came about largely by chance. His brother Jim, a popular local figure who runs a gun shop in Alfreton, lives at Carolina Farm in the hills above Tansley where he has a shooting ground. The ground has Olympic skeet, ABT, a tower and a fully automatic FITASC. Initially Joe gave just a few lessons to people who asked, but then gradually the word started to spread, until finally in November 1986 he changed his working life from dairy farming to full-time shooting instruction.

'Until then I couldn't stand watching people shoot. Now it gives me more pleasure than I could have imagined possible—I can watch our team perform for three days and be absorbed by it all. It is amazing what you can see.'

There could hardly be anyone better qualified, particularly as Joe's own career owed so much to learning. 'You have to be able to learn from others.' After early advice from Clarrie and Jack Wright, he attributes much credit for his subsequent progress to the famous German shot and coach Conrad Wernier. From 1966 to 1973 Joe used a Browning A1 skeet gun, then switched to a Rottweil designed by Wernier. He used one of the three prototypes for the next seven years, before switching again this time to a Vostok, about which he says: 'It is the most perfect skeet gun I have ever used.'

Wernier taught Joe a great deal about skeet technique. At the same time he rubbed shoulders with the world's best and his education progressed to a very high level. He did not become a high-class performer purely through shooting a lot—he actually learned skills.

His subsequent success as a coach should not, therefore, come as much of a surprise. Clients come from all over the world: in the month prior to my visit he had visitors from India, Hong Kong and America, and he was booked solid for the two months to follow. While he does undertake skeet tuition, it is general coaching which accounts for much of his work. Sporting shooters represent the biggest percentage, and quite a lot of game shooters as well. 'I think one of the most important reasons why I have been so busy is that I actually take all the lessons myself.'

Just like the days when he was winning major competitions, he is also able to provide the kind of undivided concentration which brings results. His commitment and enthusiasm are certainly infectious. His style of shooting is very uncomplicated, and based largely upon an individual's ability to respond to instinct. By using good stance, balance and consistently good gun-mount, he reckons that most people should be able to enjoy a decent success rate without worrying about forward allowance, ballistics and other technicalities—though he does have some very firm views on guns, their style, fit, weight and balance.

He is a great believer in 'shooting with the eyes', and argues that most misses are due to people taking their eyes off the target. 'When someone says they have missed behind, it is because they have temporarily moved their sight from target to the barrel. They double-check before they shoot.'

So what are the other most common flaws? 'With skeet shooters, it will be poor visual contact on the target, lack of balance and a failure to move the hand and eye together. For sporting and game shooters, there is a great incidence of people shooting off-balance. I call them lean-leaders.' He laughed as he explained what he meant, and most of us do it at some time or other: it is the habit of unwittingly following a bird to the point where the shoulder drops and the body goes off its natural balance.

'A miss will result, as the gun rolls off a bird—sporting shooters are terrible for it. You can't play any sport unless you are perfectly balanced.'

The advice is simple and uncomplicated, but you know it makes sense. Coming from a man who instructs instructors (Joe regularly gives lessons to other coaches) it is also unerringly accurate. Just like the man himself.

Further Reading

Arthur, R. *The Shotgun Stock* (A.S. Barnes & Co New York, 1971)

Askins Col, C. *Wing & Trap Shooting* (Macmillan, 1922)

Bentley, P. *Clay Target Shooting* (A. & C. Black, 1987)

Bidwell, J. & Scott, R. *Move Mount Shoot* (Crowood, 1990)

Bogardus, A. *Field Cover & Trap Shooting* (Published Author, 1881.
    Reprinted Wolfe Pub, 1987, Av. Gunnerman)

Braun, Lee. *Skeetshooting* (Benjamin Co, 1975)

Braun, Lee. *Trapshooting* (Benjamin Co, 1975)

Brister, R. *Shotgunning, Art & Science* (Winchester Press, 1977)

Broomfield, B. & Cradock, C. *Shotguns on Test* (Burlington, 1980)

Buckell, Teasdale. *Experts on Guns & Shooting* 1900
    (Reprinted Ashford Press, 1986)

Chapel, E. *Field Skeet & Trap Shooting* (Chapman & Hall, 1950)

Churchill, R. *How to Shoot* (Geofrey Bles, 1925)

Cradock, C. *A Manual of Clayshooting* (Batsford, 1983)

Cradock, C. *Cradock on Shotguns* (Batsford, 1989)

Croft, P. *Clay Shooting* (Ward Lock, 1990)

Eley. *Layouts for Clay Target Shooting* (Eley, 1971)

Etchen, F. *Common Sense Shotgun Shooting* (Standard Publications, 1946)

Gallwey, Payne. *A Modern Shooting School* (Badminton Magazine, 1896)

Hartman, B. *Hartman on Skeet* (D. Van Nostrand, 1967)

Hoare, Tony. *Successful Clay Pigeon Shooting (Crowood Press, 1991)*

ICI. *Gunning without Game* (Kynoch Press, 1938)

King, J. *Clay Pigeon Shooting* (Sportsman Press, 1991)

Lancaster, C. *Art of Shooting* 14 editions (Lancaster & Co, 1889/1985.
    Reprinted Ashford Press, 1985)

Lind, Ernie. *Complet Book Trick and Fancy Shooting* (Winchester, 1972)

Macfarland, F. *Clay Pigeon Shooting* (P. Marshall, 1964)

Midalski, E. *Clay Target Games* (Winchester Press, 1978)

Mills, D. & Barnes, M. *Amateur Gunsmithing* (Boydell Press, 1986)

Misseldine, F. *Shoot Better at Trap and Skeet* (Winchester Press, 1972)

Nobel. *A Handbook on Clay Target Shooting* (Nobel Industries, 1927)

Nobel. *The Versatile Clay Bird* (Nobel Industries, 1921)

Page, T. *The Art of Shooting Flying* (Cruse Norwich, 1785)

Raymont, M. & Jones, C. *Modern Clay Pigeon Shooting*
    (English Country Life, 1974)

Reynolds, M. & Barnes, M. *Shooting Made Easy* (Crowood, 1986)

Rose, M. & Stewart, Jackie. *Eley Book of Shooting* (Eley, 1979)

Smith, Lon. *Better Trap Shooting* (E.P. Dutton, 1931.
    This book has the famous photos by Quayle showing Shot String.

Stewart, J. *Jackie Stewart Book of Shooting* (Harper Collins, 1991)

Index